S0-BJH-583

The Library

Colby Junior College

COLBY JUNIOR COLLEGE FOR WOMEN
PARATI · SERVIRE
MENS · ANIMUS
CORPUS
1837

SCOPE OF TOTAL ARCHITECTU

WORLD PERSPECTIVES . *Volume Three*

Planned and Edited by RUTH NANDA ANSHEN

SCOPE OF
TOTAL ARCHITECTURE

BY WALTER GROPIUS

New York

HARPER & BROTHERS PUBLISHERS

SCOPE OF TOTAL ARCHITECTURE

*Copyright, 1943, 1949, 1952,
1954, 1955, by Walter G. Gropius*

Approach: Copyright, 1937, by F. W. Dodge
Corporation. *My Conception of the Bauhaus
Idea:* Copyright, 1937, by F. W. Dodge Corporation. *A Way Out of the Housing Confusion:*
Copyright, 1938, by F. W. Dodge Corporation.
Is There a Science of Design: Copyright, 1947,
by American Federation of Arts.

Printed in the United States of America

All rights in this book are reserved.

*No part of the book may be used or reproduced
in any manner whatsoever without written permission except in the case of brief quotations
embodied in critical articles and reviews. For
information address Harper & Brothers
49 East 33rd Street, New York 16, N.Y.*

FIRST EDITION

A-E

WORLD PERSPECTIVES

35572

Library of Congress catalog card number: 54–12179

Contents

CONTENTS

Illustrations

World Perspectives

WORLD PERSPECTIVES is dedicated to the concept of man born out of a universe perceived through a fresh vision of reality. Its aim is to present short books written by the most conscious and responsible minds of today. Each volume represents the thought and belief of each author and sets forth the interrelation of the changing religious, scientific, artistic, political, economic and social influences upon man's total experience.

This Series is committed to a re-examination of all those sides of human endeavor which the specialist was taught to believe he could safely leave aside. It interprets present and past events impinging on human life in our growing World Age and envisages what man may yet attain when summoned by an unbending inner necessity to the quest of what is most exalted in him. Its purpose is to offer new vistas in terms of world and human development while refusing to betray the intimate correlation between universality and individuality, dynamics and form, freedom and destiny. Each author treats his subject from the broad perspective of the world community, not from the Judaeo-Christian, Western, or Eastern viewpoint alone.

Certain fundamental questions which have received too little consideration in the face of the spiritual, moral and political world crisis of our day, and in the light of technology which has released the creative energies of peoples, are treated in these books. Our authors deal with the increasing realization that spirit and nature are not separate and apart; that intuition and reason must regain their importance as the means of perceiving and fusing inner being with outer reality.

Knowledge, it is shown, no longer consists in a manipulation of man and nature as opposite forces, nor in the reduction of data to mere statistical order, but is a means of liberating mankind from the destructive power of fear, pointing the way toward the goal of the rehabilitation of the human will and the rebirth of faith and confidence in the human person. The works published also endeavor to reveal that the cry for patterns, systems and authorities is growing less insistent as the desire grows stronger in both East and West for the recovery of a dignity, integrity and self-realization which are the inalienable rights of man who may now guide change by means of conscious purpose in the light of rational experience.

Other vital questions explored relate to problems of international understanding as well as to problems dealing with prejudice and the resultant tensions and antagonisms. The growing perception and responsibility of our World Age point to the new reality that the individual person and the collective person supplement and integrate each other; that the thrall of totalitarianism of both right and left has been shaken in the universal desire to recapture the authority of truth and of human totality. Mankind can finally place its trust not in a proletarian authoritarianism, not in a secularized humanism, both of which have betrayed the spiritual property right of history, but in a sacramental brotherhood and in the unity of knowledge, a widening of human horizons beyond every parochialism, and a revolution in human thought comparable to the basic assumption, among the ancient Greeks, of the sov-

ereignty of reason; corresponding to the great effulgence of
the moral conscience articulated by the Hebrew prophets;
analogous to the fundamental assertions of Christianity; or to
the beginning of a new scientific era, the era of the science of
dynamics, the experimental foundations of which were laid by
Galileo in the Renaissance.

An important effort of this Series is to re-examine the
contradictory meanings and applications which are given
today to such terms as democracy, freedom, justice, love,
peace, brotherhood and God. The purpose of such inquiries
is to clear the way for the foundation of a genuine *world*
history not in terms of nation or race or culture but in terms
of man in relation to God, to himself, his fellow man and the
universe, that reach beyond immediate self-interest. For the
meaning of the World Age consists in respecting man's hopes
and dreams which lead to a deeper understanding of the basic
values of all peoples.

Today in the East and in the West men are discovering that
they are bound together, beyond any divisiveness, by a more
fundamental unity than any mere agreement in thought and
doctrine. They are beginning to know that all men possess the
same primordial desires and tendencies; that the domination
of man over man can no longer be justified by any appeal to
God or nature; and such consciousness is the fruit of the
spiritual and moral revolution through which humanity is now
passing.

World Perspectives is planned to gain insight into the meaning of man, who not only is determined by history but who
also determines history. History is to be understood as concerned not only with the life of man on this planet but as
including also such cosmic influences as interpenetrate our
human world.

This generation is discovering that history does not conform to the social optimism of modern civilization and that the organization of human communities and the establishment of justice, freedom and peace are not only intellectual achievements but spiritual and moral achievements as well, demanding a cherishing of the wholeness of human personality and constituting a never-ending challenge to man, emerging from the abyss of meaninglessness and suffering, to be renewed and replenished in the totality of his life. "For as one's thinking is, such one becomes, and it is because of this that thinking should be purified and transformed, for were it centered upon truth as it is now upon things perceptible to the senses, who would not be liberated from his bondage." [1]

There is in mankind today a counterforce to the sterility and danger of a quantitative, anonymous mass culture, a new, if sometimes imperceptible, spiritual sense of convergence toward world unity on the basis of the sacredness of each human person and respect for the plurality of cultures. There is a growing awareness that equality and justice are not to be evaluated in mere numerical terms but that they are proportionate and analogical in their reality.

We stand at the brink of the age of the world in which human life presses forward to actualize new forms. The false separation of man and nature, of time and space, of freedom and security, is acknowledged and we are faced with a new vision of man in his organic unity and of history offering a richness and diversity of quality and majesty of scope hitherto unprecedented. In relating the accumulated wisdom of man's spirit to the new reality of the World Age, in articulating its thought and belief, *World Perspectives* seeks to encourage a

[1] *Maitri Upanishad* 6.34.4, 6.

renaissance of hope in society and of pride in man's decision as to what his destiny will be.

The experience of dread, in the pit of which contemporary man has been plunged through his failure to transcend his existential limits, is the experience of the problem of whether he shall attain to being through the knowledge of himself or shall not, whether he shall annihilate nothingness or whether nothingness shall annihilate him. For he has been forced back to his origins as a result of the atrophy of meaning, and his anabasis may begin once more through his mysterious greatness to re-create his life.

In spite of the infinite obligation of men and in spite of their finite power, in spite of the intransigence of nationalisms, and in spite of spiritual bereavement and moral denigration, beneath the apparent turmoil and upheaval of the present, and out of the transformations of this dynamic period with the unfolding of a world-consciousness, the purpose of *World Perspectives* is to help quicken the "unshaken heart of well-rounded truth" and interpret the significant elements of the World Age now taking shape out of the core of that un-dimmed continuity of the creative process which restores man to mankind while deepening and enhancing his communion with the universe.

New York, 1955   RUTH NANDA ANSHEN

Preface

CREATION and love of beauty are elemental for the experience of happiness. A time which does not recognize this basic truth does not become articulate in the visual sense; its image remains blurred, its manifestations fail to delight.

Since my early youth I have been acutely aware of the chaotic ugliness of our modern man-made environment when compared to the unity and beauty of old, preindustrial towns. In the course of my life I became more and more convinced that the usual practice of architects to relieve the dominating disjointed pattern here and there by a beautiful building is most inadequate and that we must find, instead, a new set of values, based on such constituent factors as would generate an integrated expression of the thought and feeling of our time.

How such a unity might be attained to become the visible pattern for a true democracy—that is the topic of this book. It is based, essentially, on articles and lectures written—with a few exceptions—during my years in Harvard University as chairman of the Department of Architecture (1937–1952).*

WALTER GROPIUS

* Acknowledgment: The idea to publish this book originated with my wife, Ise, née Frank, who undertook to edit and select the material from my manuscripts.

SCOPE OF TOTAL ARCHITECTURE

Introduction*

ENTERING a new chapter in my life that—contrary to the normal expectation of life after seventy—looks to me just as turbulent and perilous as the period preceding it, I realize that I am a figure covered with labels, maybe to the point of obscurity. Names like "Bauhaus Style," "International Style," "Functional Style" have almost succeeded in hiding the human core behind it all, and I am eager, therefore, to put a few cracks into this dummy that busy people have slipped around me.

When, as a young man, I received the first public attention I was rather put out to find my mother depressed and disapproving of the fact that my name had begun to appear in newspapers. Today I understand her apprehension all too well, because I have experienced that, in our era of fast printing and categorizing, publicity is likely to be tied around an individual like a label around a bottle. Every so often I feel a strong urge to shake off this growing crust so that the man behind the tag and the label may become visible again.

I have been told that a tree which is supposed to bear my name is to be planted in Chicago on the campus of the Michael Reese Hospital, for which I have been architectural consultant for the last eight years. I want this to be a tree in

* From a speech made by the author on the occasion of his seventieth birthday on invitation of the Illinois Institute of Technology, Chicago, May, 1953.

which birds of many colors and shapes can sit and feel sustained. I do not wish to restrict it to species with square tail-ends or streamlined contours or international features or Bauhaus garb. In short, I wish it to be a hospitable tree from which many songs should be heard, except the fake sounds of the bird imitators.

When I was a small boy somebody asked me what my favorite color was. For years my family poked fun at me for saying, after some hesitation, *"Bunt ist meine Lieblingsfarbe,"* meaning: "Multicolored is my favorite color." The strong desire to *include* every vital component of life instead of excluding part of them for the sake of too narrow and dogmatic an approach has characterized my whole life. It is, therefore, with considerable disgust that I have watched the confusing battle of words that has arisen around the representatives of the various schools of modern design. These esthetic battles are usually not stirred up by the architects themselves, but by those well-meaning or ill-meaning, self-appointed critics who, in the attempt to buttress their own esthetic or political theories, wreak havoc with the work of creative people by capturing and abusing some of their statements without comprehending the background and context they sprang from.

I have found throughout my life that words and, particularly, theories not tested by experience, can be much more harmful than deeds. When I came to the U.S.A. in 1937 I enjoyed the tendency among Americans to go straight to the practical test of every newborn idea, instead of snipping off every new shoot by excessive and premature debate over its possible value, a bad habit that frustrates so many efforts in Europe. This great quality should not get lost in favor of biased theorizing and fruitless, garrulous controversy at a moment when we need to muster all our strength and originality in trying to keep creative impulses active and effective against the deadening effect of mechanization and overorganization that is threatening our society.

Of course, the relative position which a searching mind has to take when going off the beaten path exposes it to attacks from all directions. In my time I have been accused by the Nazis of being a Red, by the Communists of being a typical exponent of the capitalistic society, and by some Americans of being a "foreigner," unacquainted with the democratic way of life. All these labels, applied to the same person, show the confusion that is caused in our time by an individual who just insisted on forming his own conviction. I look upon these temporary tempests in my personal life with the detachment that comes from experience. I know that the strong currents of our times might have cast my boat on the rocks many times unless I could have trusted my own compass.

But the thing I do not want to seem detached about is our common plight of losing control over the vehicle of progress that our time has created and that is beginning to ride roughshod over our lives. I mean that the misuse of the machine is creating a soul-flattening mass mind, which levels off individual diversity and independence of thought and action. Diversity is, after all, the very source of true democracy. But factors of expediency like high-pressure salesmanship, organizational oversimplification and moneymaking as an end in itself have surely impaired the individual's capacity to seek and understand the deeper potentialities of life.

Democracy is based on the interplay of two contrasting manifestations. On the one hand it needs diversity of minds, resulting from intensive, individual performance; on the other it needs a common denominator of regional expression, springing from the cumulative experience of successive generations who gradually weed out the merely arbitrary from the essential and typical. As irreconcilable as these two manifestations may seem to be, I believe that their fusion can and must be brought about or we shall end up as robots.

One of the U.S. Supreme Court Justices once discussed the substance of democratic procedure and I was highly interested to hear him define it as "essentially a matter of *degree*." He did not base his decisions on abstract principles of right and wrong, but wanted to consider every case in its particular circumstances and relative proportion, because he felt that it was the soundness of the whole social structure that mattered and that what might contribute to its detriment today might be inconsequential tomorrow under changing conditions, and vice versa.

To sharpen this sense of balance and feeling for equipoise is something we all have to accomplish individually in our lives. For instance, when we accuse technology and science of having deranged our previous concepts of beauty and the "good life," we would do well to remember that it is not the bewildering profusion of technical mass-production machinery that is dictating the course of events, but the inertia or the alertness of our brain that gives or neglects to give direction to this development. For example, our generation has been guilty of producing horrors of repetitious housing developments, all done on a handicraft basis, which can easily compete in deadly uniformity with those ill-advised prefabrication systems which multiply the whole house instead of only its component parts. It is not the tool, it is our mind that is at fault. The art of accurately knowing the degree to which our individual instincts are to be curbed or encouraged or our common policies enforced or resisted is apparently the privilege of few wise people, and we are desperately in need of them. No other generation has had to face so vast a panorama of conflicting tendencies and our heritage of overspecialization does not equip us too well to cope with them. The architecture we produce will inevitably reveal the degree to which we have been able to show respect for the developing social pattern which we are part of, without devitalizing our individual contribution to it.

I want to rip off at least one of the misleading labels that I and others have been decorated with. There is no such thing as an "International Style," unless you want to speak of certain universal technical achievements in our period which belong to the intellectual equipment of every civilized nation, or unless you want to speak of those pale examples of what I call "applied archeology," which you find among the public buildings from Moscow to Madrid to Washington. Steel or concrete skeletons, ribbon windows, slabs cantilevered or wings hovering on stilts are but impersonal contemporary means—the raw stuff, so to speak—with which regionally different architectural manifestations can be created. The constructive achievements of the Gothic period—its vaults, arches, buttresses and pinnacles—similarly became a common international experience. Yet, what a great regional variety of architectural expression has resulted from it in the different countries!

As to my practice, when I built my first house in the U.S.A. —which was my own—I made it a point to absorb into my own conception those features of the New England architectural tradition that I found still alive and adequate. This fusion of the regional spirit with a contemporary approach to design produced a house that I would never have built in Europe with its entirely different climatic, technical and psychological background.

I tried to face the problem in much the same way as the early builders of the region had faced it when, with the best technical means at their disposal, they built unostentatious, clearly defined buildings that were able to withstand the rigors of the climate and that expressed the social attitude of their inhabitants.

Our present responsibility seems to be to determine which features of our vast industrial civilization represent the best and lasting values and should therefore be cultivated to form the nucleus for a new tradition. Proper distinction of cultural values can, of course, develop only through steadily improved education. One of the major jobs falling to us architects in the field of cultural education would be to point up and make precise the new values and sift them from the welter of ascending and fading fashions and a mass production process that has yet to discover that change, as such, does not necessarily bring improvement. Amidst a vast production and an almost limitless choice of goods and types of all description, we need to remember that cultural standards result from a selective process of seeking out the essential and typical. This voluntary limitation, far from producing dull uniformity, should give many individuals a chance to contribute their own individual variation of a common theme and so help to evolve again the integrated pattern for living that we abandoned with the advent of the machine age. The two opposites—individual variety and a common denominator for all—will then once more be reconciled to each other.

WALTER GROPIUS

I.

Education

of Architects

and Designers

I.

Approach*

MY intention is not to introduce a, so to speak, cut and dried "Modern Style" from Europe, but rather to introduce a method of approach which allows one to tackle a problem according to its peculiar conditions. I want a young architect to be able to find his way in whatever circumstances; I want him independently to create true, genuine forms out of the technical, economic and social conditions in which he finds himself instead of imposing a learned formula onto surroundings which may call for an entirely different solution. It is not so much a ready-made dogma that I want to teach, but an attitude toward the problems of our generation which is unbiased, original and elastic. It would be an absolute horror for me if my appointment would result in the multiplication of a fixed idea of "Gropius architecture." What I do want is to make young people realize how inexhaustible the means of creation are if they make use of the innumerable modern products of our age, and to encourage these young people in finding their own solutions.

I have sometimes felt a certain disappointment at being

* From a statement, made for *The Architectural Record*, at the start of my teaching career as Professor of Architecture at Harvard University, May, 1937.

asked only for the facts and tricks in my work when my interest was in handing on my basic experiences and underlying methods. In learning the facts and tricks, some can obtain sure results in a comparatively short time, of course; but these results are superficial and unsatisfactory because they still leave the student helpless if he is faced with a new and unexpected situation. If he has not been trained to get an insight into organic development no skillful addition of modern motives, however elaborate, will enable him to do creative work.

My ideas have often been interpreted as the peak of rationalization and mechanization. This gives quite a wrong picture of my endeavors. I have always emphasized that the other aspect, the satisfaction of the human soul, is just as important as the material, and that the achievement of a new spatial vision means more than structural economy and functional perfection. The slogan "fitness for purpose equals beauty" is only half true. When do we call a human face beautiful? Every face is fit for purpose in its parts, but only perfect proportions and colors in a well-balanced harmony deserve that title of honor: beautiful. Just the same is true in architecture. Only perfect harmony in its technical functions as well as in its proportions can result in beauty. That makes our task so manifold and complex.

More than ever before is it in the hands of us architects to help our contemporaries to lead a natural and sensible life instead of paying a heavy tribute to the false gods of make-believe. We can respond to this demand only if we are not afraid to approach our work from the broadest possible angle. *Good architecture should be a projection of life itself and that implies an intimate knowledge of biological, social, technical and artistic problems.* But then—even that is not enough. To make a unity out of all these different branches of human activity, a strong character is required and that is where the means of education partly come to an end. Still, it should be our highest aim to produce this type of men who are able to visualize an entity rather than let themselves get absorbed too early into the narrow channels of specialization. Our century has produced the expert type in millions; let us make way now for the men of vision.

2.

My Conception of the Bauhaus Idea*

Aim. After I had already found my own ground in architecture before the First World War, as is evidenced in the Fagus Building of 1911 and in the Cologne Werkbund Exhibition in 1914 (Germany), the full consciousness of my responsibility as an architect, based on my own reflections, came to me as a result of the First World War, during which my theoretical premises first took shape.

After that violent eruption, every thinking man felt the necessity for an intellectual change of front. Each in his own particular sphere of activity aspired to help in bridging the disastrous gulf between reality and idealism. It was then that the immensity of the mission of the architect of my own generation first dawned on me. I saw that, first of all, a new scope for architecture had to be outlined, which I could not hope to realize, however, by my own architectural contributions alone, but which would have to be achieved by training and preparing a new generation of architects in close contact with modern means of production in a pilot school which must succeed in acquiring authoritative significance.

* See: *The New Architecture and the Bauhaus* by W. Gropius, Faber & Faber, London, 1935. "Education towards Creative Design" by W. Gropius, *American Architect and Architecture,* New York, May 1937. "The Gropius Symposium" in *The American Academy of Arts and Sciences, Arts and Architecture,* California, May, 1952.

I saw also that to make this possible would require a whole staff of collaborators and assistants, men who would work, not as an orchestra obeying the conductor's baton, but independently, although in close co-operation to further a common cause. Consequently I tried to put the emphasis of my work on integration and co-ordination, inclusiveness, not exclusiveness, for I felt that the art of building is contingent upon the co-ordinated teamwork of a band of active collaborators whose co-operation symbolizes the co-operative organism of what we call society.

Thus the Bauhaus was inaugurated in 1919 with the specific object of realizing a modern architectonic art, which like human nature was meant to be all-embracing in its scope. It deliberately concentrated primarily on what has now become a work of imperative urgency—averting mankind's enslavement by the machine by saving the mass-product and the home from mechanical anarchy and by restoring them to purpose, sense and life. This means evolving goods and buildings specifically designed for industrial production. Our object was to eliminate the drawbacks of the machine without sacrificing any one of its real advantages. We aimed at realizing standards of excellence, not creating transient novelties. Experiment once more became the center of architecture, and that demands a broad, co-ordinating mind, not the narrow specialist.

What the Bauhaus preached in practice was the common citizenship of all forms of creative work, and their logical interdependence on one another in the modern world. Our guiding principle was that design is neither an intellectual nor a material affair, but simply an integral part of the stuff of life, necessary for everyone in a civilized society. Our ambition was to rouse the creative artist from his other-worldliness and to reintegrate him into the workaday world of realities and, at the same time, to broaden and humanize the rigid, almost exclusively material mind of the businessman. Our conception of the basic unity of all design in relation to life was in diametric opposition to that of "art for art's sake" and the much more dangerous philosophy it sprang from, business as an end in itself.

This explains our concentration on the design of technical products and the organic sequence of their processes of manufacture, which gave rise to an erroneous idea that the Bauhaus had set itself up as the apotheosis of rationalism. In reality, however, we were far more preoccupied with exploring the territory that is common to the formal and technical spheres, and defining where they cease to coincide. The standardization of the practical machinery of life implies no robotization of the individual but, on the contrary, the unburdening of his existence from much unnecessary dead weight so as to leave him freer to develop on a higher plane.

All too often, our real intentions have been and still are misunderstood, namely, to see in the movement an attempt at creating a "style" and to identify every building and object in which ornament and period style seem to be discarded as examples of an imaginary "Bauhaus Style." This is contrary to what we were aiming at. *The object of the Bauhaus was not to propagate any "style," system or dogma, but simply to exert a revitalizing influence on design.* A "Bauhaus Style" would have been a confession of failure and a return to that devitalizing inertia, that stagnating academism which I had called it into being to combat. Our endeavors were to find a new approach which would promote a creative state of mind as designers at the same time, was made

g: **Preliminary Course.** The Bauhaus
ing of people possessing artistic talents as
try and handicrafts, as sculptors, painters
complete co-ordinated training of all handi-
ue and in form, with the object of teamwork
d as the basis. The fact that the man of today
tset, left too much to traditional specialized
h merely imparts to him a specialized knowl-
not make clear to him the meaning and purport
nor the relationship in which he stands to the
e—was counteracted at the Bauhaus by putting
nning of its training not the "trade" but the
ing" in his natural readiness to grasp life as a
basis of its training was a preliminary course,
g the pupil to the experience of proportion and scale,
ght, shade and color, and allowing him at the same
ass through every stage of primitive experience with
and tools of all kinds, in order to enable him to find
where, within the limits of his natural gifts, he could
a secure footing. This training, which occupied six
s, was intended to develop and ripen intelligence, feeling
deas, with the general object of evolving the "complete
" who, from his biological center, could approach all
s of life with instinctive certainty and would no longer
aken unawares by the rush and convulsion of our "Me-
nical Age." The objection that, in this world of industrial
nomy, such a general training implies extravagance or a
ss of time does not, to my mind and experience, hold good.
n the contrary, I have been able to observe that it not only

in those taking part and which would finally lead to a new attitude toward life. To my knowledge, the Bauhaus was the first institution in the world to dare to embody this principle in a definite curriculum. The conception of this curriculum was preceded by an analysis of the conditions of our industrial period and its compelling trends.

Arts and Craft Schools. When, in the last century, the machine-made products seemed to sweep the world, leaving the craftsmen and artists in a bad plight, a natural reaction gradually set in against the abandonment of form and the submersion of quality. Ruskin and Morris were the first to set their faces against the tide, but their opposition against the machine could not stem the waters. It was only much later that the perplexed mind of those interested in the development of form realized that art and production can be reunited only by accepting the machine and subjugating it to the mind. "The Arts and Crafts" schools for "applied art" arose mainly in Germany, but most of them met the demand only halfway, as their training was too superficial and technically amateurish to bring about a real advance. The manufactories still continued to turn out masses of ill-shaped goods while the artist struggled in vain to supply platonic designs. The trouble was that neither of them succeeded in penetrating far enough into the realm of the other to accomplish an effective fusion of both their endeavors.

The craftsman, on the other hand, with the passing of time began to show only a faint resemblance to the vigorous and independent representative of medieval culture who had been in full command of the whole production of his time and who had been a technician, an artist and a merchant combined. His workshop turned into a shop, the working process slipped out of his hand and the craftsman became a merchant. The complete individual, bereaved of the creative part of his work, thus degenerated into a partial being. His ability to train and instruct his disciples began to vanish and the young apprentices gradually moved into factories. There they found themselves surrounded by a meaningless mechanization which blunted their creative instincts, and their pleasure in their own work; their inclination to learn disappeared rapidly.

Difference Between Handicrafts and Machine Work. What is the reason for this devitalizing process? What is the difference between handicraft and machine work? *The difference between industry and handicraft is due far less to the different nature of the tools employed in each, than to subdivision of labor in the one and undivided control by a single workman in the other.* This compulsory restriction of personal initiative is the threatening cultural danger of the present-day form of industry. The only remedy is a completely changed attitude toward work which, though based on the sensible realization that the development of technique has shown how a collective form of labor can lead humanity to greater total efficiency than the autocratic labor of the isolated individual, should not detract from the power and importance of personal effort. On the contrary, by giving it the possibility of taking its proper place in the work of the whole it will even enhance its practical effect. This attitude no longer perceives in the machine merely an economic means for dispensing with as many manual workers as possible and of depriving them of their livelihood, nor yet a means of imitating handwork; but, rather, an instrument which is to relieve man of the most oppressive physical labor and serve to strengthen his hand so as to enable him to give form to his creative impulse. The fact that we

have not yet mastered th
consequence, still have
argument against their
discover the most eff
energies in the orga
man of the past
speculative prelim
goods. Instead o
his abilities mu
and fused with
present the young
to descend to the
become an organ fo
others; i.e., of the arti
solve a problem of his
produces goods with m
which, although associate
deep-rooted progress in the
knowledge of the new means

What, then, must we do to g
promising approach to their f
craftsmen or architects? What tra
create in order to be able to sift out
and fit him by extensive manual an
pendent creative work within the ind
in very isolated cases have training s
with the aim of turning out this new type
to combine the qualities of an artist, a te
nessman. One of the attempts to regain co
tion and to train young students both for l

gave the pupil greater confidence, but also considerably enhanced the productiveness and speed of his subsequent specialized training. Only when an understanding of the interrelationship of the phenomena of the world around him is awakened at an early age will he be able to incorporate his own personal share in the creative work of his time.

As both the future craftsman and the future artist were subject to the same fundamental training at the Bauhaus, it had to be sufficiently broad to enable each talent to find its own way. The concentric structure of the whole training embodied all the essential components of design and technique right from the beginning, in order to give the pupil an immediate insight into the whole field of his future activities. The further training merely gave breadth and depth; it differed from the elementary "preliminary training" only in degree and thoroughness, but not in the essence. Simultaneously with the first exercises in materials and tools, the training in design commenced.

Language of Vision.   In addition to technical and handicraft training, the designer must also learn a special language of shape in order to be able to give visible expression to his ideas. He has to absorb a scientific knowledge of objectively valid optical facts, a theory which guides the shaping hand and provides a general basis on which a multitude of individuals can work together harmoniously. This theory is naturally not a recipe for works of art, but it is the most important objective means for collective work in design. It can best be explained with an example from the musical world: the theory of counterpoint which, though in the course of time it may have undergone certain changes, is, nevertheless, still a supraindividualistic system for regulating the world of tones. Its mastery is required lest the musical idea should remain lost in chaos; for creative freedom does not reside in the infinitude of the means of expression and formation, but in free movement within its strictly legal bounds. The academy, whose task it had been from its beginning—when it was still a vital force— to tend and develop this theory for the optical arts, had failed because it lost touch with reality. Intensive studies were therefore made at the Bauhaus to rediscover this grammar of design in order to furnish the student with an objective knowledge of optical facts—such as proportion, optical illusions and colors. Careful cultivation and further investigation of these natural laws would do more to further true tradition than any instruction in the imitation of old forms and styles.

Workshop Training. In the course of his training, each student of the Bauhaus had to enter a workshop of his own choice, after having completed the preliminary course. There he studied simultaneously under two masters—one a handicraft master, and the other a master of design. This idea of starting with two different groups of teachers was a necessity, because neither artists possessing sufficient technical knowledge nor craftsmen endowed with sufficient imagination for artistic problems, who could have been made the leaders of the working departments, were to be found. A new generation capable of combining both these attributes had first to be trained. In later years, the Bauhaus succeeded in placing as masters in charge of the workshops former students who were then equipped with such equivalent technical and artistic experience that the separation of the staff into masters of form and masters of technique was found to be superfluous.

The training in handwork given in the Bauhaus workshops must not be taken as an end in itself, but as an irreplaceable means of education. The aim of this training was to produce designers who were able, by their intimate knowledge of materials and working processes, to influence the industrial production of our time. An attempt was made, therefore, to produce models for the industry which were not only designed but actually made in the workshops of the Bauhaus. The creation of standard types for the articles of daily use was their main concern. These workshops were essentially laboratories in which the models for such products were carefully evolved and constantly improved. Even though these models were made by hand, the model designers had to be fully acquainted with the methods of production on an industrial scale and so, during their training, the Bauhaus sent out its best students for a time, to do practical work in factories. Inversely, skilled workmen also came from the factories into the Bauhaus workshops, to discuss the needs of industry with masters and students. In this way a mutual influence arose which found its expression in valuable products, the technical and artistic quality of which were appreciated by manufacturer and customer.

Development of Standard Types. The creation of standard types for everyday goods is a social necessity. The standard product is by no means an invention of our own era. It is only the methods of producing it which have changed. It still implies the highest level of civilization, the seeking out of the best, the separation of the essential and superpersonal from the personal and accidental. It is today more necessary than ever to understand the underlying significance of the conception "standard"—that is to say, as a cultural title of honor—and firmly to combat the shallow catchword propaganda which simply raises every industrial mass product to that high rank.

In its collaboration with industry, the Bauhaus attached special importance also to bringing the students into closer touch with economic problems. I am opposed to the erroneous view that the artistic abilities of a student may suffer by sharpening the sense of economy, time, money and material consumption. Obviously it is essential clearly to differentiate between the unrestricted work in a laboratory on which strict time limits can hardly be imposed, and work which has been ordered for completion at a certain date; that is to say, between the creative process of inventing a model and the technical process involved in its mass production. Creative ideas cannot be made to order, but the inventor of a model must nevertheless develop trained judgment of an economic method of subsequently manufacturing his model on mass production lines, even though time and consumption of material play only a subordinate part in the design and execution of the model itself.

The whole institution of the Bauhaus training shows the educational value which was attached to practical problems, which impel the students to overcome all internal and external friction. Collaboration on actual orders which the master had to execute was one of the outstanding advantages of handicrafts training in the Middle Ages. For that reason, I endeavored to secure practical commissions for the Bauhaus, in which both masters and students could put their work to a test. In particular, the erection of our own institute buildings, in which the whole Bauhaus and its workshops co-operated, represented an ideal task. The demonstration of all kinds of new models made in our workshops, which we were able to show in practical use in the building, so thoroughly convinced manufacturers that they entered into royalty contracts with the Bauhaus which, as the turnover increased, proved a valuable source of revenue to the latter. The institution of obligatory practical work simultaneously afforded the possibility of paying students—even during their three years of training—for salable articles and models which they had worked out. This provided many a capable student with some means of existence.

After a three-year training in handwork and design, the student had to submit to an examination both by the masters of the Bauhaus and by the "Chamber of Handicrafts" in order to obtain the Journeyman's Certificate. The third stage for those who wanted to proceed was the building training. Co-operation on practical building sites, practical experiments with new building materials, studies in draftsmanship and engineering in addition to design led to the Master Certificate of the Bauhaus. The students then became either practical architects or collaborators in the industry, or teachers—according to their special gifts. The thorough manual training in the workshops served as a very valuable equipment for those students who found it impossible to penetrate into the more comprehensive and complex task of the architect's profession. The gradual and manifold instruction of the Bauhaus enabled him to concentrate on precisely that kind of work which best suited his capabilities.

The most essential factor of the Bauhaus work was the fact that, with the passing of time, a certain homogeneity was evolved in all products: this came about as the result of the consciously developed spirit of collaborative work, and also in spite of the co-operation of the most divergent personalities and individualities. It was not based on external stylistic features, but rather on the effort to design things simply and truthfully in accordance with their intrinsic laws. The shapes which its products have assumed are therefore not a new fashion, but the result of clear reflection and innumerable processes of thought and work in a technical, economic and form-giving direction. The individual alone cannot attain this goal; only the collaboration of many can succeed in finding solutions which transcend the individual aspect—which will retain their validity for many years to come.

The Creative Teacher.   The success of any idea depends upon the personal attributes of those responsible for carrying it out. The selection of the right teacher is the decisive factor in the results obtained by a training institute. Their personal attributes as men play an even more decisive part than their technical knowledge and ability, for it is upon the personal characteristics of the master that the success of fruitful collaboration with youth primarily depends. *If men of outstanding artistic ability are to be won for an institute, they must from the outset be afforded wide possibilities for their own further development by giving them time and space for private work.* The mere fact that such men continue to develop their own work in the institute produces that creative atmosphere which is so essential for a school of design and in which youthful talents can develop. This is the most important supposition, to which all other questions affecting the organization must be subordinated. There is nothing more deadening to the vitality of a design school than when its teachers are compelled, year in and year out, to devote the whole of their time to classes. Even the best of them tire of this unending circle and must in time grow hardened. *Art, in fact, is not a branch of science which can be learned step by step from a book.* Innate artistic ability can only be intensified by influencing the whole being, by the example of the design master and his work. Whereas the technical and scientific subjects can be learned by progressive courses of lectures, the training in design must, to be successful, be conducted as freely as possible, at the personal discretion of the artist. The lessons which are intended to give direction and artistic incentive to the work of the individuals and groups need by no means be very frequent, but they must provide essentials which stimulate the student. The ability to draw is all too frequently confused with the ability to produce creative design. Like dexterity in handicrafts, it is, however, no more than a skill, a valuable means of expressing spatial ideas. Virtuosity in drawing and handicrafts is not art. The artistic training must provide food for the imagination and the creative powers. An intensive "atmosphere" is the most valuable thing a student can receive. Such a *"fluidum"* can only grow when a number of personalities are working together to a common end; it cannot be created by organization, nor can it be defined in terms of time.

When I tried to find out for myself why the seeds of the Bauhaus venture have not come up faster, I saw that the demands on the flexibility of human nature during the last generation have been indeed all too sweeping. With that rapid torrent of constant changes in all fields of activities—material as well as spiritual—natural human inertia could not keep pace.

Ideas of cultural import cannot spread and develop faster than the new society itself which they seek to serve. However, I think it is not an overstatement when I maintain that the community of the Bauhaus, through the wholeness of its approach, has helped to restore architecture and design of today as a social art.

3.

Is There a Science of Design?*

FOR many years I have systematically collected facts about the phenomenon of our human sight and its relation to the other senses, and about our psychological experiences with form, space and color. These are as real as any material problems of structure and economy which I shall disregard here. *I consider the psychological problems, in fact, as basic and primary, whereas the technical components of design are our intellectual auxiliaries to realize the intangible through the tangible.*

The term "design" broadly embraces the whole orbit of man-made, visible surroundings, from simple everyday goods to the complex pattern of a whole town.

If we can establish a common basis for the understanding of design—a denominator reached through objective findings rather than through personal interpretation—it should apply to any type of design; for the process of designing a great building or a simple chair differs only in degree, not in principle.

An individual of the species man has certain characteristics in common with others of his kind in the way he perceives and

* See: "Design Topics" by W. Gropius, *Magazine of Art,* December 1947.

experiences his physical world. *Most important is the fact that sensation comes from us, not from the object which we see.* If we can understand the nature of what we see and the way we perceive it, then we will know more about the potential influence of man-made design on human feeling and thinking.

Many years ago I saw a movie called *The Street.* It started with an unforgettable scene acquainting the audience in a flash with the tangled web of a matrimonial drama. First the wife, then the husband looks down from the window into the street. She sees the gray, trivial, everyday life as it is; but he projects his imagination into the scene, transforming it into a sensational picture giving brilliance, intensity and meaning to the pattern of life before his eyes.

Reality and Illusion.   I remembered this experience when I read a study by Earl C. Kelley of Wayne University about "education for what is real," as verified by recent experiments in sensation, made in co-operation with the Dartmouth Eye Institute in Hanover, New Hampshire. One of the basic statements of this remarkable study is:

> We do not get our sensations from things around us but the sensations come from us. Since they do not come from the immediate environment (the present) and obviously cannot come from the future, they come from the past. If they come from the past they must be based on experience.

The demonstration is as follows: You are presented with three peepholes about the size of the pupil of the eye. You are asked to look through these holes in turn. The material back of the holes is well lighted. In each case you see a cube, with its three dimensions and its square sides. In general, the three cubes look substantially the same. All appear to be about the same distance away [*Fig. 1*].

Then you are permitted to look back of the boards through which the peepholes run. When you do this, you see that one of the holes indeed has a wire cube back of it. Another, however, has a drawing on a plane, with scarcely any of the lines running parallel. The third is a number of strings stretched between wires running away from the eye.

Neither of the latter two look anything at all like a cube when viewed from behind the scenes. And yet the sensation in each case was a cube. . . .

Widely different materials caused the same pattern on the retina of our eye and resulted in the same sensation. The sensation could not come from the material, since in two cases it was not a cube. It could not come from the pattern on the retina since that pattern was not a cube. The cube does not exist except as we call it a cube; and that sensation did not come from the material in our environment, but from us. It came from prior experience.

Similarly a baby in the cradle, seeing the moon for the first time in his life, tries to catch it; *what is at first a mere reflected image on the retina assumes, in later life, symbolic meaning by experience*. But we need not go back to the undeveloped mind of the baby.

Subconscious Reactions.   For instance when you drive in a car on a slushy road and a passing car coming in the opposite direction hurls slush at your windshield you blink and dodge. The subconscious reactions are automatic; though our intellect tells us that the windshield protects us, the reaction to ward off possible danger for our eye reoccurs every time. Our eye obviously does not take any chances.

Imagine sitting on a balcony twenty stories high above the ground, the balcony having an open railing made of vertical bars. Though the railing gives you physical protection, you will have a sensation of giddiness if you look down. Giddiness, however, stops immediately if the railing is covered with cardboard or paper, for this enclosure then gives support to the eye. Our equilibrium is re-established through the illusion of safety although nothing has been added in fact for greater physical safety. The eye does not know, it reacts automatically.

The equivalent phenomenon in horizontal direction is the so-called agoraphobia, i.e., the dread of open spaces which seizes sensitive persons crossing a large open square (*Fig. 2*). They feel lost in a space the size of which is not in keeping with the human scale. But if some vertical planes were erected on that open space like wings on a stage, such as shrubs or fences or walls, the illusion of safety would be reinstated, and the dread would disappear; for the eyes of the person groping in space now find a frame of reference to support them; when they hit a solid in the field of vision they register its outline just as radar does.

These examples show that there is a split between physical perception on the one hand and our intellectual knowledge on the other. The subconscious stratum of our human nature obviously reacts unswervingly like a ship's compass; it is uninfluenced by any gambol of the intellect, but it is subject to illusions.

Design Education. *My thesis is that artistic creation draws its life from the mutual tension between the subconscious and the conscious faculties of our existence, that it fluctuates between reality and illusion.* The subconscious or intuitive powers of an individual are uniquely his therefore. It is futile for an educator in design to project his own subjective sensations into the student's mind. All he can do successfully is to develop his teaching on the basis of realities, of objective facts common to all of us. But the study of what is reality, what is illusion, requires a fresh mind, unaffected by the accumulated debris of intellectual knowledge. Thomas Aquinas has said, "I must empty my soul that God may enter." Such unprejudiced emptiness is the state of mind for creative conception. But our present intellectual emphasis on book education does not promote such mental climate. The initial task of a design teacher should be to free the student from his intellectual frustration by encouraging him to trust his own subconscious reactions, and to try to restore the unprejudiced receptivity of his childhood. He then must guide him in the process of eradication of tenacious prejudices and relapses into imitative action by helping him to find a common denominator of expression developed from his own observation and experience.

If design is to be a specific language of communication for the expression of subconscious sensations, then it must have its own elementary codes of scale, form and color. It needs its own grammar of composition to integrate these elementary codes into messages which, expressed through the senses, link man to man even closer than do words. The more this visual language of communication is spread, the better will be the common understanding. This is the task of education: to teach what influences the psyche of man in terms of light, scale, space, form and color. Vague phrases like "the atmosphere of a building" or "the coziness of a room" should be defined precisely in specific terms. The designer must learn to see; he must know the effect of optical illusions, the psychological influence of shapes, colors and textures, the effects of contrast, direction, tension and repose; and he must learn to grasp the significance of the human scale. Let me illustrate:

Some Biological Facts about Our Way of Seeing. As we have already seen, man perceives his physical environment by sensory experience. Our sense of vision and our tactile sense supplement each other in this highly complicated physiological act of seeing. Our retinas supply us with flat images only as the lens of a camera projects a flat picture on a sensitive film. The experience of distance in space has to be acquired by each individual personally, supported by his tactile sense. Remember the baby reaching for the moon (*Fig. 3*).

(*Fig. 4*) * The human eye is built very similar to a photographic camera.

(*Fig. 5*) The most common delusion. The human eye actually sees the environment as an inverted mirror image. By means of a psychological correction which is acquired in practice from a very early age, we turn the image around bringing it into correspondence with reality.

(*Fig. 6*) Diagrammatic section through the human eye showing the cornea lens and retina.

(*Fig. 7*) Looking into a human eye: (*a*) the accommodation muscle which turns and releases the ligaments of the lens (*b*); (*c*) the longitudinal fibers of the iris which dilate the pupil when they contract; (*d*) the circular fibers which decrease the size of the pupil when they contract. Beneath the iris is the lens, above it is the dome of the cornea.

(*Fig. 8*) The iris diaphragm of the camera compared to that of the human eye. At the left the diaphragm is contracted, at the right it is released just as in a photographic camera the contracted diaphragm sharpens the image.

(*Fig. 9*) This picture shows the adjustment of the human

* Figs. 4–11 from *Der Mensch* by Dr. Fritz Kahn, Alb. Müller Verlag, Zürich, 1939.

eye—not only of the diaphragm, but also of the lens. In the upper picture you see that the flattening out of the lens brings the sharp adjustment of the image, whereas the lower is blurred because of wrong adjustment. Technology uses the same method for reproducing and printing pictures as nature does in our eye, using a sieve or screen.

In the eye the image projected upon the retina by the lens is likewise broken up into dots by the rods and cones of the retina since each cell sees only one dot no larger than itself. Strongly stimulated cells report to the brain "light," weakly stimulated cells "dark." If a retinal image were to be magnified several hundred times, we would see that it consists of points or dots just like an enlarged piece of a halftone engraving.

(*Fig. 10*) This is the television apparatus of the human eye which like that of a broadcasting station transforms optical images into electrical currents (a, b, c), the supporting framework (g, h), the photosensitive cells (f), the connecting cells (e), the large transmitting cells (d), the nerve cable (i, k), the protecting base.

(*Fig. 11*) The human eye is a combination camera for day and night photography. The retinal cones on the left are daylight apparatus. They require much light, producing sharply defined panchromatic pictures. The rods in our eye shown on the right side are twilight apparatus. They are strongly photosensitive but produce indistinct achromatic pictures.

The curvature of the retina as well as of our eye lens is the source of certain distortions of images. This complicates further the necessary association of our space-perceiving senses and is the common cause of a wealth of optical illusions. The

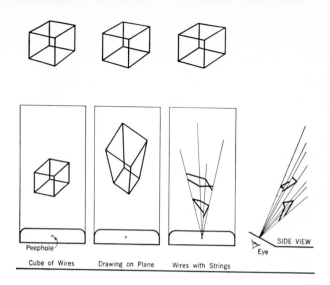

Cube of Wires   Drawing on Plane   Wires with Strings

Peephole

SIDE VIEW

Eye

Fig. 1

Fig. 2: Plaza at entry of Château de Versailles

Fig. 3: Field of vision of a nine-month-old child

Fig. 4: Photographic camera and the human eye

Fig. 5: A common delusion

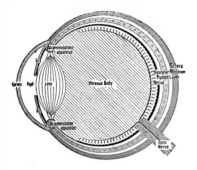

Fig. 6: Diagrammatic section through the human eye

Fig. 7: View into a human eye

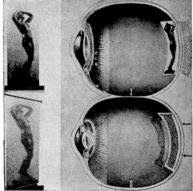

Fig. 9: The adjustment of the human eye

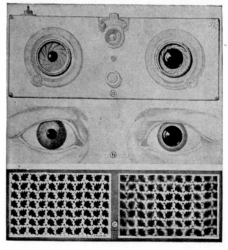

Fig. 8: The iris diaphragm of the camera and that of the human eye

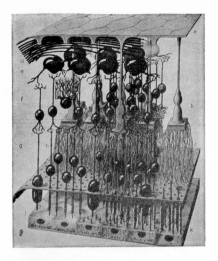

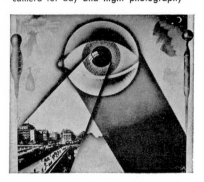

Fig. 10: The television apparatus of the human eye

Fig. 11: The human eye, a combination camera for day and night photography

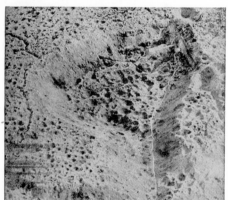

Fig. 12: Concavities of a moon landscape

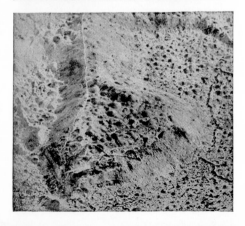

Fig. 13: The same picture upside down

Fig. 14

Fig. 16: Interior of Cathedral in Siena

Fig. 15: Girl in bathing suit

Fig. 17: Phenomenon of irradiation

Fig. 18: St. John in Lateran, Rome

Fig. 19: El Greco's "Grand Inquisitor"

Fig. 20: Analysis of Greco's picture (Bauhaus exercise)

Fig. 21: Relativity of values

Fig. 22: The size of our body is our yardstick

Fig. 23: Egyptian Sphinx

Fig. 24: Westminster Cathedral in London

Fig. 25: Indian Temple

Fig. 26: Indian Temple, close view

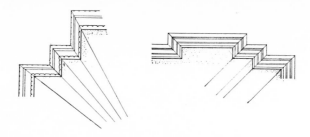

Fig. 27: Left, Indian cornice; right, Baroque cornice

Fig. 28: Plinth of the Parthenon Temple

Fig. 29: Picture by Balla, Italy, depicting motion in space

Fig. 30: Picture by Picasso, depicting profile and front of a woman's face

knowledge of these illusions appears to be indispensable for a designer.

Optical Illusions. The plainly recognizable concavities of a moon landscape (*Fig. 12*) will appear convex if we turn the picture upside down (*Fig. 13*). Note that the stream running through a valley in the original picture now runs over a crest. Our eyesight is unable to adjust this illusionary phenomenon of reciprocation to the reality of the original view now reversed. Modern abstract painters have made use of the intriguing interplay of form elements which can be read as being either convex or concave, thus giving an illusion of motion.

An accurate square, striped by parallel lines running either horizontally or vertically, appears to be elongated in the opposite direction from that of the parallel lines (*Fig. 14*). This is an important fact to know for architectural and fashion design. In addition, the width of the stripes has to be carefully chosen to be in keeping with the size of the figure. The girl in the bathing suit (*Fig. 15*) looks more slender in horizontal than vertical stripes. In the same way the columns of the cathedral of Siena, Italy, (*Fig. 16*) would appear heavier if the stripes were vertical.

Another optical phenomenon is that called "irradiation." A bright figure on dark background appears to be larger than a black figure on a bright background (*Fig. 17*). This illusion is caused by the light spilling over the dark edges of a silhouette projected on our retina. Silhouettes of sculptured figures standing against the bright sky appear to be reduced by irradiation. The volume of such sculpture has to be exaggerated in order to give the intended effect of truthfulness (*Fig. 18*). The light nibbles at the contours.

Psychological Influence of Shapes and Colors. El Greco's "Grand Inquisitor" is more than the portrait of a man. It depicts the state of mind this man evoked in the beholder and in the artist. The explosive stroke of the brush and the shapes chosen suggest horror and dread of a terrifying menace —the Inquisition (*Fig 19*).

Shapes can be exciting or soothing. In addition, their colors —shrill or soft—can increase the intended effect. Color and texture of surfaces have an effective existence of their own, sending out physical energies which can be measured. Such effect can be warm or cold, advancing or receding, bright or dark, light or heavy, in tension or in suspension, or even attractive or repulsive (*Fig. 20*). A New York designer who calls himself a color engineer reports that

> he is sure that violet induces melancholy; that yellow is an energizing color, conducive to conviviality, increased brain activity and a sense of well being, and that classrooms painted yellow are good for retarded children, while nurseries painted yellow are likely to inhibit naps; that blue induces not the "blues" but relaxation, and that old people often become "blue-thirsty," that the psychological reactions to red are stimulating to brain, pulse and appetite and that if you stand twenty feet away from a red chair and a blue chair the red chair will appear a foot closer; that green makes people feel cold and that stenographers working in green offices are prey to psychosomatic chills, which they readily shed, along with their sweaters, when, without a change of temperature, orange slipcovers are placed on their chairs or orange curtains are hung at their windows; that a charity appeal mailed in a light-blue-green envelope will command a surer philanthropic response than one sent in a white envelope; that a twenty-pound box painted dark

blue will look heavier, and seem harder to carry, than the same box painted light yellow; that a telephone bell ringing in a white booth will seem louder than the same bell ringing in a purple booth; and that a peach consumed in the dark will appear to have less flavor than one whose color is visible.*

Relativity. We can hardly believe that the gray dot in all five cases of this picture (*Fig. 21*) is of the same darkness. It shows the relativity of values. The same factual value of the gray disks appears to change with its brighter or darker background. Human nature seems to depend more than we realize on the contrast of opposites which keep us alert and alive, since they create an alternating tension or repose. Colors can be active or passive; planes or walls can be made to advance or recede by color treatment. The dimensions of a room thus appear to be different from what the actual measurement tells us. *In fact the designer—if he masters these means—can create illusions which seem to belie the facts of measurement and construction.*

What Is the Human Scale? The size of our body (of which we are always conscious) serves as a yardstick when we perceive our surroundings (*Fig. 22*). Our body is the scale unit which enables us to establish a finite framework of relationships within the infinite space. Unusual scale may have a ridiculous or a repulsive effect. One's emotional interest in an object may be altered merely by a change of its size, deviating from the expected norm.

Or emotional interest can be greatly intensified just by close-up enlargement. I remember the intense physical horror

* See: "Howard Ketchum—Color Engineer," *The New Yorker*, March 8, 1952.

I experienced once when seeing on the screen the enlarged picture of a scorpion and a mantis, appearing as huge monsters tearing each other to pieces in a gruesome life and death struggle. Merely through an enlargement of the optical scale, causing a closer emotional relation, strong physical and psychological sensations sprang up which would not have occurred had I seen the fight in its original small scale.

All this must bring us to the conclusion that it lies within the grasp of the designer to organize the psychological effects of his creation at will by increasing or decreasing its scale or that of its parts which changes the relationship with us.

When the Aztecs or the Egyptians built a pyramid their intention was to create awe and fear of God. The designer strove for an expression of the supernatural through large scale (*Fig. 23*). The Pharaohs and Caesars, playing God and intending to subjugate their subjects by fear, expressed their power by megalomaniac axes of superhuman scale. Hitler and Mussolini both received in rooms of colossal size, seated at the opposite end of the entrance; the approaching visitor was made to feel uneasy and humble.

Westminster Cathedral in London is an example of an out-of-scale building; overburdened with decorations and striped all over on top, it leaves an impression of pettiness and confusion in spite of its huge physical size. Its design has missed the right relationship to the human scale (*Fig. 24*).

Distance, Time and Space Relations. But it is not only the absolute size relation between our own body and the objects we see which has to be considered by a designer; he also must anticipate the varying distances from which the beholder may view his work. The effect of a building will be intense only when all requirements for human scale have been fulfilled for any potential distance or direction of view.

From far away its silhouette should be simple so that it can be grasped at a glance like a symbol even by an ever so primitive spectator as well as by a man passing in an automobile (*Fig. 25*). When we come closer we distinguish protruding and receding parts of the building, and their shadows serve as scale regulators for the new distance. And finally, standing close by, no longer able to see the whole edifice, the eye should be attracted by a new surprise in the form of refined surface treatment (*Fig. 26*).

Is it the result of instinctive sureness if the designer has applied the proper human scale, or that of knowledge, or does a balance of both account for it?

We know that the Indian architects first had to learn several crafts; then, in their forties, before they were permitted to build a temple, priests gave them secret training in mathematics. I wonder whether they had a science of vision. They certainly did not shrink from complicated working processes in order to achieve a desired optical effect. For instance, the miter lines of their richly molded cornices do not simply run parallel, as in Western architecture, but they meet in a distant vanishing point. This tapering off creates an optical illusion of greater depth and more impressive scale (*Fig. 27*).

For the same reasons, Iktinos, the designer of the Parthenon, which represents the culmination of perfection and subtlety in Western design, inclined its columns slightly toward the center axis of the building and delicately curved all its horizontal lines to compensate for the optical illusion of concavity; for a long, straight and horizontal line appears to cave in at its center because of the curvature of our retina. This distorts and weakens the effect. In order to counteract this illusion, the plinth of the Parthenon was raised four inches higher at its center than at its ends (*Fig. 28*). It is evident that the base was purposely built this way, for it stands on solid rock and its vertical joints are still very tight today, no settling could have displaced its original lines. Here intuition and intellect joined to triumph over the natural deficiencies of human vision. Here is true architecture.

These selected examples characterize the elements which form the language of design. What do we know about the relations of these elements in "space"? Every one of us has once in his life attempted to understand the infinite space by lying on his back, looking into the stars, thinking and trying to envisage the endlessness of the heavens, only to recognize that we are denied cognition of the infinite. The mathematician has invented the infinitely small and the infinitely large quantity. He has certain signs for them. But each is an abstraction we cannot understand. We comprehend space and scale only within a frame of reference which is finite. Confined space—open or enclosed—is the medium of architecture. The right relation between the building masses and the voids which they enclose is essential in architecture. This may appear obvious, but I have found that many people are not at all conscious of this relation, and that there are even trained architects who design only in terms of the buildings themselves, ignorant of the fact that the open spaces between them are just as important a part of the architectural composition.

Many of us still live innocently in a static three-dimensional world of Newtonian conception which has long since collapsed. Philosophers and scientists have replaced that static conception by a dynamic picture of relativity. In today's design terminology this profound change has been acknowledged by what we call "space-time" relations. Science has discovered the relativity of all human values and that they are in constant flux. There is no such thing as finality or eternal truth according to science. Transformation is the essence of life. I would like to quote a report about the Princeton Bicentennial meeting, "Planning Man's Physical Environment."

The Physical Environment which the architects were invited to consider had changed at a terrorizing velocity within their working lifetime. The expanding universe had become the exploding universe, and time, the new Fourth Dimension, had become more ponderable than any of the other three. Man had changed, too, but not enough. The architects showed that their buildings had felt the now decisive effect of Time and its mirror, Motion—but Man emerged under their inquiring stare as a creature bent by the relentless past, confused by his vestigial emotions, and so handicapped by defective vision that he literally can see only what he wants to see.

Accordingly, the element of time, introduced as a new fourth dimension, begins to penetrate human thought and creation.

The Need for Change. This shift in the basic concept of our world from static space to continuously changing relations engages our mental and emotional faculties of perception. Now we understand the endeavors of Futurists and Cubists who first tried to seize the magic of the fourth dimension of time by depicting motion in space (*Fig. 29*). In a picture by Picasso the profile and front of a face are depicted; a sequence of aspects is shown simultaneously (*Fig. 30*). Why? This element of time, apparent in modern art and design, evidently

35572

increases the intensity of the spectator's reactions. The designer and the artist seek to create new and stimulating sensations which will make us more receptive and more active. This statement corresponds with Sigmund Freud's findings that irritants generate life. Primitive cells kept in a solution, perfect in temperature and nourishment, slowly die in contentment; but if an irritating agent is added to the liquid they become active and multiply.

The English historian Toynbee tells a story of a ship's captain who won reputation by always bringing in the freshest herring. On his deathbed he gave away his secret, namely, that he had always put a catfish into the boat's fish tank. The catfish killed a few, frightened them all and thereby kept them in splendid condition. Similarly human beings receive new stimulation from irritants. *Art must satisfy this perpetual urge to swing from contrast to contrast; the spark, generated by tension of opposites, creates the peculiar vitality of a work of art.* For it is a fact that a human being needs frequently changing impressions in order to keep his receptive abilities alert. Unchanging conditions, perfect as they may be, have a dulling and lulling effect. To give a trivial example: A whole day's traveling in an air-conditioned Pullman car of evenly adjusted temperature, air velocity and humidity makes us uneasy. Even if it is a very hot day we like to step out at a station, seeking the contrast of less comfortable conditions, for this will enable us to enjoy again the comfortable air-conditioning back in the car. Our functions of adaptation have called for a contrast.

This need for change becomes very evident when we compare the psychological effects of daylight with those of artificial light. Recently I came across this statement in the Illuminating Engineering Society's *Report of the Committee on Art Gallery Lighting:* "Today any interior (museum) gallery can be artificially lighted to better effect than is possible by daylight; and, in addition, it can always reveal each item in its best aspect, which is only a fleeting occurrence under natural lighting." A fleeting occurrence! Here, I believe, is the fallacy; for the best available artificial light trying to bring out all the advantages of an exhibit is, nevertheless, static. It does not change. Natural light, as it changes continuously, is alive and dynamic. The "fleeting occurrence" caused by the change of light is just what we need, for every object seen in the contrast of changing daylight gives a different impression each time.

For instance, imagine the surprise and animation experienced when a sunbeam, shining through the stained glass window in a cathedral, wanders slowly through the twilight of the nave and suddenly hits the altarpiece *(Fig. 31)*. What a stimulus for the spectator, though experiencing only a "fleeting occurrence." I remember a vivid experience I once had in the Pergamon Museum in Berlin. To me the light on the temple walls, coming from skylights, seemed to be too diffused and uniform. But one night I happened to drop in when a photographer with a large spotlight was at work. I was electrified by the effect of the strong direct illumination which brought the reliefs to life all of a sudden and helped me discover a new beauty of the sculptures which I had never observed before.

One day we may have at our disposal man-made moving sunlight to be used at will, varying in quantity, intensity and color. However, as long as artificial light cannot yet fully comply with our requirements, I believe that we should not exclude the dynamic qualities of daylight as supplement to artificial lighting wherever it is feasible because it satisfies our need for change. To give you an example of the psychological means at our disposal to keep our senses alert and responsive I shall try to analyze what could be done to make a visit to a museum into a stimulating instead of an exhausting experience. As we know, the capacity of a visitor to receive the messages of many masterpieces, crowded together, will dwindle rapidly unless we are able to refresh him frequently. His mind must be neutralized after each impression before a new impression can sink in. We cannot keep him in a high pitch of ecstasy for hours while he is wandering through a gallery, but the acuity of his interest can be kept awake by skillful design offering him ever varying space and light effects and an arrangement of display that is rich in contrasts. Only if he is thus compelled to use his natural functions of adaptation from tension to repose will he remain an untired and active participant. The arrangement of the exhibition spaces themselves and the distribution of exhibits in them should create a sequence of arresting surprises which must be well timed and properly scaled to fit the visitor's susceptibility. With this demand we enter the realm of architectural creation.

It is evident that motion in space, or the illusion of motion in space produced by the artist's magic, is becoming an increasingly powerful stimulant in contemporary works of architecture, sculpture, painting and design. In architecture today there is a preference for transparency, achieved through large areas of glass and through undercutting and opening parts of the building. This transparency aims at producing the illusion of a floating continuity of space. The buildings seem to hover, space seems to move in and out (*Fig. 32*). Sections of the infinite outdoor space become part of an architectural

Fig. 31

Fig. 32: Corner of the Bauhaus Building

Fig. 33: Living room of House Poissy by Le Corbusier

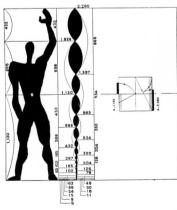

Fig. 34: Diagram of the Modulor by Le Corbusier

space composition which does not stop at the enclosing walls, as in past periods, but is carried beyond the building into its surroundings. Space seems to be in motion (*Fig. 33*).

Common Denominator for Design. Educators in design have started to bring new order into the findings of philosophy and science. A basic philosophy of design needs first of all a denominator common to all. Some of the initial groundwork in the formulation of a language of design has been done by the Bauhaus, by Le Corbusier and Ozenfant in *L'Esprit nouveau,* by Moholy-Nagy in his *The New Vision* and *Vision in Motion,* by the teachings of Josef Albers, by Kepes's *Language of Vision,* by Herbert Read's *Education Through Art* and particularly by Le Corbusier's *Modulor* (*Fig. 34*) and by others in these and related fields.

Will we succeed in establishing an optical "key," used and understood by all, as an objective common denominator of design? This can, of course, never become a recipe or a substitute for art. *Intellectual art is sterile, and no work of art can be greater than its creator. The intuitive directness, the short cut of the brilliant mind, is ever needed to create profound art. But an optical key would provide the impersonal basis as a prerequisite for general understanding and would serve as the controlling agent within the creative act.*

4.

Blueprint of an Architect's Education[*]

A. GENERAL EDUCATIONAL BACKGROUND

I BELIEVE that every healthy human being is capable of conceiving form. The problem seems to me not at all one of existence of creative ability but more one of finding the key to release it.

This problem is not America's problem alone; but it is perhaps more acute in this country because Americans, in their great enthusiasm for learning, are likely even to outdo Europeans in their efforts to cultivate their receptive and reproductive abilities to such a degree that creative instincts sometimes become submerged. This is not true with respect to the creative and inventive spirit in the technical field. Here the living generation seems to have no difficulty at all in encouraging bold pioneering and proud disregard of standards set by the past. But people behave altogether differently in their attitude toward the arts. Our great heritage seems to have left us stunned and bereft of original impulse and, from being participators and creators, we have changed into connoisseurs

[*] See: "Training the Architect" by W. Gropius, *Twice A Year*, Number 2, 1939, New York. *"Plan pour un enseignement de l'Architecture"* by W. Gropius, *L'Architecture d'Aujourd'hui*, Paris, February, 1950.

and scholars. If we investigate the vague feelings of the average man toward the arts, we find that he is timid and that he has developed a humble belief that art is something which has been invented centuries ago in countries like Greece or Italy and that all we can do about it is to study it carefully and apply it. There is no natural, eager response to the works of modern artists who try to solve contemporary problems in a contemporary way, but, rather, a great uneasiness and a strong disbelief that they can turn out something worthy of the great works of their forefathers.

This surprising sterility is in my opinion due not so much to inborn lack of ability or interest, but is a result of the fact that we are today separated into two groups of beings—the "public" and the "expert." Each person feels that he is an "expert" in one or two fields and just the "public" in all the others. But you know, probably, from experience that no one is able really to appreciate any display of ability in any field if he, himself, has not to a certain degree taken part in its problems and difficulties at some time. But the way art and design are taught today to the average youngster often does not give him any clue toward contemporary problems and contemporary tasks. He emerges from school and college filled to the brim with knowledge, but he has rarely been engaged in the task of meeting himself. I think we have been exceedingly successful so far in working out ways of acquainting our children with the achievements of the past, but I do not think we are as successful in stimulating them to come forth with their own ideas. We have made them study art history so hard that they have found no time to express their own ideas. By the time they have grown up they have developed such fixed ideas of what art is that they have ceased to think of it as of something to be freely approached and recreated by themselves. They have lost the joyful, playful urge of their early youth to shape things into new forms and have become, instead, self-conscious onlookers. This, however, is not the fault of the individual but seems to have been caused by the social changes in life.

The Origin of Abstract Art.   When, in the great art periods of former times—say, in the Middle Ages—an artist painted a Madonna, he was immediately understood by every-body on account of the common, established social and reli-gious background of his contemporaries. Today we are living between two civilizations: the old one went to pieces, the new one is just in the making. An artist of today can be understood only by a clique, not yet by the whole community, as the spiritual content of our civilization is not yet so firmly settled that it may be clearly symbolized by the artist. This may give us also a clue to what brought about the so-called "abstract art" of today whose discoveries have so deeply influenced architecture. The community, being deprived of the old stand-ards of social and religious ideals, confined the artist to isola-tion. He lost touch with the life of the community. His way out of this dilemma was his attempt to concentrate on the very medium of his art, observing and discovering new phe-nomena in space and color, and abstaining from any literary content in his work. Naturally, art became severed from the life of the people. That is what we have to face today.

Balance Between Experience and Book Knowledge.   I am convinced, though, that in every human being there are artistic faculties; the deeper values of life, however, are being impaired today by putting the emphasis of our existence on secondary considerations: business as an end in itself and this or that practical occupation. The "trade-mentality," so to speak, has superseded the desire for a balanced life as it informed former periods. Our whole system of education is directed to fit the man as soon as possible for specialized work. As soon as the happy playtime of the child is over he becomes confined to only one sector of life, losing more and more his innate connection with the totality of life. Discrepancy between occupation and vocation is seriously increasing. The courage to venture into other fields of human experience has vanished in our specialized system of production with its almost exclusively material aims. No doubt education has suffered considerably from our overestimation of material aspects and of a one-sided intellectual approach. Good education, aiming at preparing the individual for a creative attitude and for equipoise in life, must certainly lead him beyond mere fact information and book knowledge into direct personal experience and action. We must give our young people more opportunity to acquire such personal experience during their educational training, for only if we make them "find" facts by themselves can knowledge turn into wisdom.

It is characteristic of the current trend that most influential educational plans published in recent years treat the visual arts rather casually, not at all as a discipline belonging to the central core of education. *We seem to have forgotten that, since time immemorial, creative esthetic disciplines in the arts have always generated ethic qualities. We are too overconfident of the benefits from intellectual training. Art, being the product of human desire and inspiration, transcends the realms of logic and reason. It is a field of interest common to all, as beauty is a basic requirement for civilized life.*

The true aim of all education—too often forgotten, however

—is to stimulate enthusiasm toward greater effort. I am convinced that "safety first" is a foul slogan for a young man. The idea of personal security, being in itself an illusion, breeds irresponsibility and egoism. It is a mere materialistic conception. *No durable result in any trend of education can be expected without a dominating ideal, the human or social component of which has to direct the professional one—not vice versa.* Although such an aim may appear self-evident, it has become extremely rare in today's educational practice. Surely a student must be fitted for practical life, but the opposite danger of educating dreamers, secluded from the world, is hardly imminent today. The overemphasis on fact-knowledge, on intellectual reasoning has obviously carried our generation astray. It has lost touch with the totality of life and with its social implications. Intuitive quality—eternal source of all creative action—is being underrated. We see our youth mistrusting their own instincts and denying everything which cannot be conclusively reasoned. In my opinion they should, instead, be encouraged to be heedful of their emotions, learning to control rather than to subdue them. They need spiritual guidance beyond professional practicalities to develop their own creative substance, not only their intellect. The greater the spiritual aims, the better youth will conquer material difficulties. *When intuition has found food, skill develops most rapidly while routine alone can never supersede creative vision. Highest reality can be given shape only by a being who has comprehended sublimest unreality.*

B.   CURRICULUM

Creative Design.   *In all great creative periods, archi-tecture in its highest embodiment has been the dominating mother of all arts, has been a social art.*   I therefore believe that the architecture of the future is destined to dominate a far more comprehensive sphere than it does today. Today our architectural education is far too timid, overemphasizing scholarly discipline and almost solely directed toward the so-called "Fine Arts" and toward the past. An esthetic con-ception, so to speak, has fatally displaced a creative conception of art. Creative art and history of art should no longer be confused. "Creating new order" is the artist's task; that of the historian, to rediscover and explain orders of the past. Both are equally indispensable, but they have entirely different aims. Successful teaching of creative design cannot therefore be handled by historians but only by a creative artist who is a "born teacher."

The architect of the future should create through his work an original, constructive expression of the spiritual and ma-terial needs of human life, thus renewing the human spirit instead of rehearsing thought and action of former times. He should act as a co-ordinating organizer of broadest experience who, starting from social conceptions of life, succeeds in integrating thought and feeling, bringing purpose and form to harmony.

If we expect the future architect to be as many-sided as that, what must his preparation be?

Art in the Nursery.   If we start from the conviction that each healthy individual is originally capable of producing form, the optical sense should be developed already in early childhood. We must remember that the child's urge to play leads to experiment and invention, source of all sciences and of all arts. Training must be started therefore in nurseries and kindergartens, giving the children abundant opportunity to build, model, draw and paint in a very free form, as in play, which is intended to attract the child and to stimulate his imagination.

Art in School. Creativeness in the growing child must be awakened through actual working with all kinds of materials in conjunction with training in free design. Throughout the whole duration of the school manual skill and form perception are to be trained simultaneously by "building" (with actual materials), assembling, modeling, painting, free-hand and geometrical drawing. But this is important: *no copying, no elimination of the urge to play, i.e., no artistic tutelage!* The whole task of the teacher is constantly to stimulate the child's imagination and his desire to build and draw. The child's drawings and models must not even be corrected, for his power of imagination is too easily irritated by grownups if we impose our own wider knowledge too much upon him. Knowledge of facts is indispensable, of course, but it must be taught with sufficient respect toward the younger being's specific imagination, which differs from our own and which tends to find new expression. Imperceptibly guiding the child during the very difficult transition from play to work, the teacher—besides giving it the scientific facts and technical advice—must encourage him again and again by trying to stimulate his indigenous inspiration.

Professional Training in Design. Upon leaving school, the young student—planning to become an architect or designer —has arrived at that crossroads where a decision is due: either to follow the long way of higher education or to go directly into professional training. Here he urgently needs most thoughtful and careful advice. Is his character, his talent, his vision, his perseverance so strong, so promising that he should aim at becoming an independent architect or should he train himself rather to be a skilled draftsman? In order to diminish the number of false decisions made in this respect a sort of qualification test should be passed by all—a test of creativeness and power of imagination. All those students, who, possessing artistic talent, have passed the qualification test at the beginning of their training—also those who started first in a technical school—should then be offered a higher training in universities and schools of design.

Method of Teaching. For this part of his training consistency of approach in his studies is imperative. Overwhelmed by the profusion of contradictory opinions about the world at large as they are offered by institutions of higher learning he is in danger of becoming apathetic or cynical unless his educators present him with a very definite and, as it were, unilateral curriculum which should not change its direction until a certain maturity is reached and a conviction has been formed. The objection that such a consistent method would be too one-sided is not valid, for only he who has understood really well one way of thinking will be able later to compare it to other ways of thinking and to select elements from them intelligently for his own creative attempts.

The teaching of a method of approach is more important than the teaching of skills. It should be a continuing process which must grow concentrically like the annual rings of a tree. In all its stages the scope should be all-embracing instead of sectional, increasing slowly in intensity and detail in all fields of discipline simultaneously. The integration of the whole range of knowledge and experience is of the greatest importance right from the start; only then will the totality of aspect make sense in the student's mind. He will easily absorb all further details and place them where they belong if he progresses from the whole to the details, and not vice versa.

Such an educational approach would start the student off into a creative effort toward integrating simultaneously design, construction and economy of any given task with its social ends. Obvious as this demand appears to be from an intellectual point of view, educational experience has shown that it takes years to bring the student into the habit of simultaneously conceiving all three—design, construction and economy —as an inseparable and interdependent entity. The reason for the widespread sectional approach in architectural education seems to be the overemphasis on intellectual academic training and the resulting lack of opportunity for experience in field and workshop. I cannot see why knowledge alone should be made the primary object of education, when direct experience is just as indispensable as a basis for subsequent training. Paper has become too exclusive a medium of exchange. The book and the drafting board cannot give that invaluable experience gained by trial and error in the workshop and on the building site. Such experience should therefore be interwoven into the training right from the start, not added on later, after the academic part of learning has been already completed. For practical experience is the best means of guaranteeing a synthesis of all the emotional and intellectual factors in the student's mind; it prevents him from rushing off into "precocious" design, not sufficiently weighted down by the know-how of the building process. No doubt the fatal separation between craftsmanship and academic learning during the development of the machine age has split architecture from building. The problem of how to co-ordinate both—scientific knowledge and field experience—is crucial in our educational system. I will try to outline, therefore, a plan which might help to correct these present deficiencies, starting off first with a suggestion for a more scientific approach in design.

The general indolence of people toward the arts and architecture and the prevalent methods of education in design seem to be interdependent. Through improved education people should be encouraged to believe again in the basic importance of art and architecture for their daily lives. But so long as we consider the problems involved to be a matter of individual feelings which cannot be objectively defined as to standards of value, we cannot expect them to be recognized as basic for educational progress. *The spiritual implications of art in society are to be redefined and, with the help of the scientists and using their methods of precision, the social and psychological components of art—not only the technical ones —are to be determined by a distinct order of values and meanings.*

Common Denominator of Design.   Basic order in design needs first of all a denominator common to all, derived from facts. A common language of visual communication will give the designer a foundation of solidarity for his spontaneous expression in art; it will free him from the sad isolation from which he is suffering at present since, in a socially disrupted world, we have lost the common key for understanding the visual arts.

In music a composer still uses a musical key to make his composition understood. Within the framework of only twelve notes the greatest music has been created. Limitation obviously makes the creative mind inventive.

In architecture the "golden means," the "modules" of the Greeks, the "triangulation" of the Gothic builders give evidence that in the past also optical keys have existed, serving as common denominators for the working teams of early builders.

For a long period, however, no common denominator has guided our expression in the visual arts. But today, after a long, chaotic period of *"l'art pour l'art,"* a new language of vision is slowly replacing individualistic terms like "taste" or "feeling" with terms of objective validity. Based on biological facts— both physical and psychological—it seeks to represent the impersonal cumulative experience of successive generations. Here roots true tradition.

Language of Vision. In modern architecture and design there is a reawakening toward a language of vision. We are able today to feed the creative instinct of a designer with richer knowledge of visual facts, such as the phenomena of optical illusion, of the relation of solids and voids in space, of light and shade, of color and of scale; objective facts instead of arbitrary, subjective interpretation or formulas long since stale.

Order of course can never become a recipe for making art. The artist's inspirational spark transcends logic and reason. But a language of vision derived from old and new discoveries in science controls his creative act. It provides simultaneously the common key for understanding the artist's message and transforms its paradoxical content into visible terms of expression.

Yet before it can become common to all, it must be made valid through general education. This goal cannot be reached by theoretical knowledge alone; it must be combined with continuous practical experience.

Emphasis on Practical Experience.   Emotional faculties cannot be trained by analytical methods but only by creative disciplines as in music, poetry and the visual arts. Making is certainly not a mere auxiliary to thinking. It is a basic experience indispensable for the unity of purpose within the creative act. It is the only educational means which interrelates our perceptive and inventive faculties.

If we compare teaching the arts of design in the past with our present methods of training, the discrepancy becomes apparent at a glance. In the past, design was developed from apprenticeship in workshops—today, from the platonic drafting board. What used to be an auxiliary only for the maker of things—paper design—has become the central discipline of the designer. This shift of emphasis from learning by doing to intellectual discipline is typical of the present educational methods in design. But can an architect become a master of his craft without previous experience with tools and materials, without the know-how of an illuminating experience in building and making? Should architectural education then be separated from its present academic framework? Many architects would agree with a decisive turn toward greater emphasis on practical experience. I, personally, have grave doubts as to whether the present bookish climate of universities can offer at all a healthy breeding ground for architects. The impact of industrialization on our profession has been so decisive that the young generation of designers should be trained in close touch with the building industries and with their laboratories. As such a desirable change develops slowly, however, I shall attempt here to outline a transitional curriculum which, making use of existing academic facilities, aims at balancing academic learning by direct experiences in the workshop and on the building site.

Experimental Workshop and Preliminary Design Course. A continuous training of basic manual skill in experimental workshops combined with disciplines in the fundamentals of surface, volume and space, and of composition—derived from objective findings—must be developed on all levels of general and professional education. Both the reinstatement of workshop practice and the introduction of scientific courses leading to a common language of visual communication are basic requirements for successful teaching of the arts of design and especially of architecture.

This training should start with a general preliminary course aimed at co-ordinating the elements of handwork and design. As the beginner does not yet know the relationship in which he stands to the world at large, it would be wrong to put the "trade" idea or any specialization at the beginning of his training. *In his natural readiness to grasp life as a whole a student should first get a comprehensive view of the vast field of possibilities for expression lying before him.* The customary training in mere drawing is not sufficient as a preparation. Drawing and painting are certainly most valuable means of self-expression, but paper, pencil, brush and water color are not enough to develop the sense of space so necessary to freedom of expression. The student should be introduced first, therefore, to three-dimensional experiments; that is, to the elements of "building," i.e., composition in space with all sorts of experiments in materials. For example, observing the contrast between rough and smooth, hard and soft, tension and repose, will help the student to discover for himself by exercise of his hands the peculiarities of materials, their structure and textures. Working with materials, the student begins simultaneously to understand surface, volume, space and color. In addition to technical skill, he develops his own form language in order to be able to give visible expression to his ideas. After he has absorbed the elementary studies, he should then be ready to attempt compositions of his own invention.

The aim of such design work is to widen the personality rather than to provide professional skill. Its success will depend greatly on the qualities of the teacher who, by encouraging and stimulating, must release the student's own imagination, must oppose with objectivity any reproduction or imitation of other people's conceptions, including his own. The student will then experience his own ability for making creative short cuts which go beyond his preceding intellectual research.

Such a training will give confidence and independence and will thus enhance the productiveness and speed of any subsequent professional training.

Professional Training. After such preliminary experience the professional designer can then start his specialized curriculum from solid ground. Still he will need the workshop and the building site all along, to relate his design to the realities of materials and techniques. It is then that he will realize that his knowledge of the language of vision, his skill in construction, in draftsmanship and representation are all indispensable implements for expressing the all-important social end of his creative effort.

Field Practice. In educational practice, the best means of preserving the unity of the entire training on all levels is to relate it to as many realistic experiences as possible. The problems given should be built up on real conditions, suggesting an actual site and calling in a "client." The more the collaboration between teachers and students resembles office practice, the better. Visiting buildings under construction, manufacturing plants, research institutes will stimulate the student's imagination and strengthen his understanding of making and building. But most important, he should work as an apprentice on a building under construction or as an assistant to its clerk-of-the-works, in order to learn to cope with the elements of the building process, the assembly of building parts and the potential frictions between the various subcontractors. How can a student understand flashing and roofing via the drafting board, or the economical and technical problems involved in the sequence of the building process merely from drawings? In practice only, closely observing the procedure of executing a building from drawings, will he gather experience which will make sense to him. Knowledge collected by others and handed out to him theoretically remains a contention without proof in his mind; he can learn by experience only and not by authority. Every student, before applying for a professional degree, should therefore see a building being constructed from start to finish; such experience should be made obligatory.

In addition to such field practice, graduate schools should run a laboratory workshop in connection with a sample collection. Here, experiments should be made by teachers and students together for the finish of interior and exterior parts of buildings—textures and colors—and of their relations in space. As the practical part of the architect's profession is highly technical, he should be given opportunities for experimenting and testing similar to those given to students of medicine, biology and chemistry in their laboratories.

History of Art and Architecture. Studies in the history of art and architecture, intellectual and analytical in character, make the student familiar with the conditions and reasons which have brought about the visual expression of the different periods: i.e., the changes in philosophy, in politics and in means of production caused by new inventions. Such studies can verify principles found by the student through his own previous exercises in surface, volume, space and color; they cannot by themselves, however, develop a code of principles to be valid for present creation in design. Principles have to be established for each period from new creative work. History studies are therefore best offered to older students who have already found self-expression. When the innocent beginner is introduced to the great achievements of the past, he may be too easily discouraged from trying to create for himself. As soon as he has found his bearings, however, through self-expression in workshop and studio, history studies are a welcome means of refining his thinking without luring him into an imitative attitude. These studies should be started in the third year, instead of in the first year of training.

I sum up my conclusions for a transitional approach in architectural education:

1. The architect is to be a co-ordinator—a man of vision and professional competence—whose business it is to unify the many social, technical, economic and artistic problems which arise in connection with building.

The architect has to recognize the impact of industrialization and should explore the new relationships dictated by the social and scientific progress.

2. In an age of specialization, method is more important than information. The training of an architect should be concentric rather than sectional. In essence it should be all-inclusive throughout its duration, gaining in certainty of approach—that is, in clearness of thought and in the know-how of its realization. It should aim at teaching the student that it is through a creative attitude and independence of conception that he will arrive at basic convictions, not by accepting ready-made formulas.

Most essential is the unity of educational purpose. Man is to be the focus; his spiritual and material needs in relation to the life of the community should determine all stages of the student's training.

2a. The approach toward any kind of design—of a chair, a building, a whole town or a regional plan—should be essentially identical not only in respect to their relationship in space but to social aspects as well. The common ideal to which all are addressed should be emphasized above their material and technical means of realization; for all products of design are to be part of the organic whole, part of our man-made environment in town and country.

3. Three-dimensional conception is the basic architectural discipline. Methods of stimulating interest in visual expression in all fields of the plastic arts must train the student first to see, to perceive distance, and to grasp the human scale. Such disciplines are indispensable for acquiring the instinctive sureness to organize three-dimensional space and to conceive it simultaneously in terms of structural efficiency, economy of means and harmony of appearance.

4. Knowledge will come to life only by individual experience. Therefore, designing and building—the drafting board and the job—should be closely related on all levels. Field practice should not be added on as a separate experience, after an academic training of several years' duration has been completed. It should be an integral part of the curriculum itself.

5. In the first year, basic design-and-workshop practice combined should introduce to the students the elements of construction and of "building" by developing three-dimensional exercises to be carried out with materials and tools. At the same time a design course, incorporating actual problems, should focus all activities of the group on the social aim of improving the life of the community. Elements of planning are to be included in these comprehensive initial studies.

6. In the second and third year, the design-and-construction studio, supplemented by field experience during the summer vacations and by activities in a laboratory, will correlate further experience with the broadening knowledge. The term "field experience" does not refer to work in an office, but to practice directly in the field, as an assistant to the foreman or the supervisor. This field experience—not less than six months—should be made obligatory for any professional degree in architecture. It should include also acquaintance with the building industry.

7. Construction should be taught as part and parcel of design, for both are directly interdependent. Equal emphasis must be put on both; no student should be promoted so long as he is deficient in either one. Design and construction problems should be related to actual conditions regarding the site and the requirements for the use of the building. They should

be approached as inseparable from the problems of the community which include the all-important factors of economy.

8. The students should be trained to work in teams—also with students of related techniques—in order to learn methods of collaboration with others. This will prepare them for their vital task of becoming co-ordinators of the many individuals involved in the conception and execution of planning and building projects. The nature of teamwork will lead the students to good well-co-ordinated architecture rather than to flashy "stunt" design.

9. History studies should be started in the third year rather than in the first, to avoid intimidation and imitation. They should help the maturer students to analyze the origin of masterworks of the past and to show him how the architectural conception of a past period, as evident from the remaining examples, resulted from its religion, its social setup and its means of production.

10. Teachers should be appointed only after sufficient practical experience of their own, both in design and building. The trend to engage young men as teachers who have just completed an academic training is harmful. For only teachers with broad experience can muster the desirable resourcefulness so necessary to stimulate the student consistently all along. The best education can offer is stimulation, for it makes the student eager to use his own initiative. Every teacher in architecture and engineering should have the right to private practice, for this alone can replenish his resourcefulness. Without such opportunity, he is bound to dry out rapidly and then withdraw to an "authoritative" platform.

11. Schools of architecture of smaller size—say, with an enrollment of 100 or 150 students—are more efficient than

large ones. The most valuable intangible of a school, an intensive "atmosphere," results from mutual participation of faculty and students in all activities; this is easily lost in oversized schools so adverse to intimate group effort.

12. The efficiency of teaching performance depends on the number of students per teacher. An architect's training calls for individual coaching in order to help the student on terms adapted to his own personal talent and state of development. An overburdened teacher will be lost to all of his students. The desirable number of students per teacher should be twelve to sixteen at the most.

The emphasis in all my arguments is on the creative factor. That is, that a program of search rather than research makes the creative architect. Such a program, I believe, will lead our potential architects from observation to discovery to invention and finally to an intuitive shaping of our contemporary scene.

II.

The Contemporary Architect

5.

Appraisal of the Development of
Modern Architecture*

TODAY we are in a position to prove conclusively that the outward forms of modern architecture are not the whim of a few architects hungry for innovation, but the inevitable consequential product of the intellectual, social and technical conditions of our age. It has taken a quarter of a century of earnest and pregnant struggle to bring these forms into being—forms which evince so many fundamental structural changes when compared with those of the past. I think the present situation can be summed up as follows: a breach has been made with the past which enables us to envisage a new aspect of architecture corresponding to the technical civilization of the age we live in; the morphology of dead styles has been destroyed and we are returning to honesty of thought and feeling; the general public, which was formerly indifferent to everything to do with building, has been shaken out of its torpor; personal interest in architecture as something that concerns every one of us in our daily lives has been aroused in wide circles; and

* See: "The Formal and Technical Problems of Modern Architecture and Planning" by W. Gropius, *Journal of the Royal Institute of British Architects*, London, May 19, 1934.

the lines of future development have become clearly manifest throughout Europe.

But this development has encountered obstacles: confusing theories, dogmas and personal manifestoes; technical difficulties and finally the dangers arising from formalistic will-o'-the-wisps. The worst of all of these was that modern architecture became fashionable in several countries! Imitation, snobbery and mediocrity have distorted the fundamentals of truth and simplicity on which this renaissance was based. Spurious phrases like "functionalism" and "fitness for purpose equals beauty" have deflected appreciation of the new architecture into minor and purely external channels. This one-sided characterization is reflected in that frequent ignorance of the true motives of its founders, and a fatal obsession which impels superficial people to try to relegate this phenomenon to one isolated province instead of perceiving that it is a bridge which unites opposite poles of thought.

The idea of rationalization, which many people aver is the outstanding characteristic of the new architecture, is only its purifying role. The other aspect, the satisfaction of the human soul, is just as important as the material. Both find their counterpart in that unity which is life itself. The liberation of architecture from the mass of ornament, the emphasis on the functions of its structural members and the quest for concise and economical solutions, only represent the material side of that formalizing process on which the practical value of the new architecture depends. *What is far more important than this structural economy and its functional emphasis is the intellectual achievement which has made possible a new spatial vision—for whereas the practical side of building is a matter of*

*construction and materials, the very nature of architecture
makes it dependent on the mastery of space.*

The transformation from manual to machine production
so preoccupied humanity for a century that instead of pressing
forward to tackle the real problems of design, men were long
content with borrowed styles and formalistic decorations.

This state of affairs is over at last. A new conception of
building, based on realities, has developed; and with it has
come a new and changed perception of space. The very
different appearance of the numerous good examples of the
new architecture which already exist exemplify these changes
and the new technical means we now use to express them.

How far has the struggle progressed in the meantime, and
what parts have the various nations played in it? I will begin
with the precursors of the prewar era, and confine myself to
contrasting the actual founders of the new architecture up to
1914: Berlage, Behrens, myself, Poelzig, Loos, Perret, Sullivan
and St. Elia; and drawing up a brief balance of their joint
achievement. The governing factors in my choice will be, not
the esthetics of the buildings concerned, but the degree of
independence and creative achievement with which in these
buildings their architects have definitely enriched the movement. With one exception this choice is based not on paper
projects, but executed designs: a consideration which seems
to me of some importance.

Germany played the leading rôle in the development of the
new architecture. Long before the war the Deutscher Werkbund had been formed in Germany. At that time such an
outstanding leader as Peter Behrens was not a strange or
isolated phenomenon. On the contrary, he already had a
powerful backing in the Deutscher Werkbund, a body which

formed a reservoir of the forces of progress and renewal. I well remember the animated discussion at the Werkbund's public sessions during the Cologne Exhibition of 1914 which so many foreigners attended; and the publication of the first of the Werkbund's well-known yearbooks at about the same time. It was in active collaboration in the latter that I gained my first comprehensive insight into the movement as a result of drawing up a sort of inventory of the existing state of architecture. Between 1912 and 1914, too, I designed my first two important buildings: the Fagus Factory at Alfeld, and the Office Building for the Cologne Exhibition, both of which clearly evince that emphasis on function which characterizes the new architecture.

During this same prewar period Auguste Perret was the leading personality in France. The Théâtre des Champs Elysées in Paris, built in 1911–13, was designed by Perret in collaboration with the Belgian Van de Velde, who was then living in Weimar and working in close contact with the Deutscher Werkbund. Perret's chief title to fame is his extraordinary constructive skill, which altogether surpasses his gifts as spatial designer. Although more engineer than architect, he indubitably belongs to the founders of modern architecture, for it was he who succeeded in freeing architecture from its ponderous monumentalism by his audacious and wholly unprecedented forms of construction. Yet this great pioneer for long remained a voice crying in the wilderness as far as France was concerned.

In Austria, Otto Wagner had built his Post Office Savings Headquarters in Vienna at the turn of the century. Wagner dared to expose plain surfaces entirely free of decoration and moldings. Today, it is almost impossible for us to imagine what a revolution such a step implied. Simultaneously Adolph Loos, another Viennese, began writing those articles and books in which he set forth the fundamentals of the new architecture, and building that large shop in the Michaelplatz, immediately opposite the Hofburg in Vienna, which so inflamed the passions of a population accustomed to Baroque forms.

In 1913 Futurism was launched in Italy, of which St. Elia, who unfortunately died in the war, was one of the leading adherents. At the 1933 Triennial Exhibition in Milan his memory was invoked by Marinetti, the founder of Futurism, as one of the great originators of the new architecture. St. Elia wrote astonishingly accurate anticipations of the ideology of the coming architecture, but he never had a chance to carry out any practical work. His project for a skyscraper on a four-tiered street remained a paper design.

In Holland development was slower. Berlage, De Bazel and Lauweriks, who based their work on anthropological premises, had reanimated the use of geometrical systems in design, and had also, in emulation of those important English pioneers, Ruskin and Morris, inspired a revival of handicrafts. A romantic mystical school continued in Holland until well into the postwar decade. It was in 1917, three years after the Cologne Exhibition, that the group known as "Stijl" was formed, of which Oud and Van Doesburg became the leaders. In 1914 the most advanced buildings in Holland were Berlage's office buildings and De Klerk's housing blocks.

In the United States the revival of architecture had begun as far back as the eighties, simultaneously with the development of a new constructional technique.

Root built a brick skyscraper in Chicago in 1883. About the end of the century Sullivan—Frank Lloyd Wright's far too little recognized master—constructed buildings of this type which are epoch-making, and also formulated architectural principles which contain the pith of the functional doctrines of today. We must not forget that it was Sullivan who wrote, "Form should follow function." Intellectually speaking, he was more articulate in his ideas than Frank Lloyd Wright, who was later to inspire so many European architects in both a spatial and a structural sense. Later on, and more particularly in the postwar period, Frank Lloyd Wright began to manifest a growing attachment to romanticism in his lectures and articles that was in sharp contradiction to the European development of the new architecture. At the present moment the Americans have the most fully developed constructional technique of any nation in the world—as I had an opportunity of seeing for myself in the course of my investigations in the United States. But in spite of Sullivan and Frank Lloyd Wright and a very highly developed technical organization, their artistic evolution has remained in abeyance. The intellectual and cultural background necessary for its preparation does not as yet exist.

This outlines the most important development in the period prior to the war. The war intervened, but at its close the new architecture blossomed forth simultaneously in several centers. The most organic and continuous progress was made in Germany, where the leaders of the movement were all moving spirits in the Deutscher Werkbund, and a wide circle of supporters was soon found to share their views. In 1919 the Bauhaus was founded at Weimar, and later on its practical influence on housing developments in the cities with its marked social effect became apparent. Thereafter the movement began to be welcomed by public authorities at large.

Fig. 35: Originators of the new architecture up to 1914

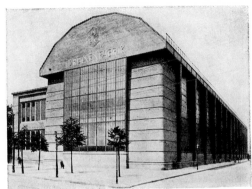

1910: Behrens

1906: Sullivan

1910: Loos

1911: Gropius

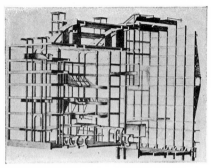

1911-1913: Perret

1911: Poelzig

1913: St. Elia

1914: Berlage

In Holland the "Stijl" movement began to take root; Oud, Rietveld, and Van Loghem built their first buildings, and the City of Amsterdam its extensive housing estates. The "Stijl" movement had a marked effect as propaganda, but it over-emphasized formalistic tendencies, and so provided the impulse that made "cubic" forms fashionable. The structural concepts of the new architecture are now beginning to oust the theories which inspired the Dutch Modernists.

About the same time, the French-Swiss Corbusier, who had studied for a time under Peter Behrens, began to work in France. In 1916 he was still using pilasters and cornices, but shortly afterward he started to edit *L'Esprit Nouveau,* and to produce architectural and literary work of an astonishingly wide scope which made a profound impression on the young generation in every country. But in contrast to Germany, where a whole following had sprung up in and around the Bauhaus, the movement in France developed only as the purely personal concern of a few individuals; and people in general remained indifferent, with the result that no new school arose as a logical result of their activities.

Switzerland produced a number of capable architects after the war who considerably influenced the movement, more particularly in regard to town planning.

The Stockholm Exhibition of 1930 was an important success for the new architecture in the Scandinavian countries.

England's contribution has been confined to housing and town planning; but Sir Raymond Unwin's ideas and the English garden cities have influenced the whole European housing movement.

Bourgeois accomplished useful pioneering work in Belgium, and has taken a successful part in the replanning of Brussels.

Vigorous young groups have been formed in Czechoslovakia, Poland, Spain and England; while a very active Japanese group exists at Osaka.

In the United States, the Austrian Neutra and the Dane Lönberg-Holm, who have made their home there, and who are both men of outstanding initiative and energy, are carrying on the movement. The younger generation of Americans, some of whom studied at the Bauhaus, are slowly beginning to find their bearings and evolve their own formal components.

The appearance of co-operative working groups, to which I have just drawn attention, is characteristic of the latest development of the new architecture. In countries which might be supposed to have least in common with one another similar free organizations of young architects have been formed, roughly speaking, on the Bauhaus model, who collaborate in practical and experimental work. I consider this co-operative principle particularly promising, and very appropriate to the spirit of our age; especially when these groups include engineers and economists. Such groups—when led by men who possess the right qualifications for holding their members together and inspiring the team spirit—are a guarantee for the thoroughness and many-sidedness of the work produced, as each member inspires his fellow. But groups of this kind must be founded on a voluntary basis. It is impossible to run them within the usual frame of rules and regulations.

An international organization based on the same principles called "Les Congrés Internationaux d'Architecture Moderne" (CIAM) was formed in Switzerland; to which twenty-seven national groups have since adhered. The objects of the congress are to pool the experience of the different countries, and to co-ordinate the results so as to provide practical data and sound directives for town planning and to insure their recognition and adoption in the various countries. This orientation of the congress work is not, of course, accidental, but represents a direct continuation of the original principles of the new architecture applied to the larger unit of the town. The conception which the new kind of architect has of his calling, as that of a co-ordinating organizer, whose business it is to resolve all formal, technical, sociological and commercial problems and combine them in a comprehensive unity, has inevitably extended his researches beyond the house to the street, from the street to the more complete organism which is the city itself; and ultimately into the wider field of regional and national planning. I believe that the future development of the new architecture is bound to embrace these wider spheres, and concern itself with all their congruent details; and that it must inevitably progress toward an ever fuller conception of the province of design and construction as one vast indivisible whole whose roots are embedded in life itself.

In the face of these proofs of the genuineness of the movement no one who takes the trouble to investigate its sources can possibly still maintain that it is based on an antitraditional obsession for technique qua technique which blindly seeks to destroy deeper loyalties and is doomed to lead to the deification of pure materialism. The order by which it seeks to restrict arbitrary caprice is the result of a most thorough social, technical and artistic investigation. *I believe that our conception of the new architecture is nowhere in opposition to that of tradition; since respect for tradition does not imply an esthetic preoccupation with bygone forms of art, but is, and always has been, a struggle for essentials—that is to say, a struggle to get at what is at the back of all technique, which is forever seeking visible expression with its help.*

6.

Archeology or Architecture for Contemporary Buildings?*

ARCHITECTURE is said to be a true mirror of the life and social behavior of a period. If that is true, we should be able to read from its present features the driving forces of our own time. There is conflicting evidence, however. If we compare current public buildings—for example, the "classical" character of the National Gallery in Washington—with the contemporary character of the new group of buildings for the United Nations, a deep-seated controversy becomes apparent.

We will find an even more puzzling discrepancy if we observe the current state of collegiate architecture, which is bound, of course, to influence the next generation growing up in and around it.

Should it follow the Gothic tradition or the Georgian tradition or should it fulfill the requirements of new college buildings by using "modern" means of expression unprejudiced by any period design? And, if this last trend seems to have become more prevalent in recent years, why is that so? What is happening to tradition? What stand will finally be

* This article, published in the *New York Times Magazine* of October 23, 1949, under the title "Not Gothic But Modern for Our Colleges," received the Howard Myers Memorial Prize in 1951.

taken by responsible educators? These questions seem to touch the very roots of our civilization, laying open both its weaknesses and its virtues.

Good original architecture depends just as much on an understanding public as on its creators.

Vasari tells the revealing story of Brunelleschi's cathedral in Florence and how the entire population participated in its development. People get the kind of architecture they are ready for, and tendencies in education which foster either creative habits or imitative habits are decisive in forming their attitude.

One of the consequences of our purely analytical and intellectual approach to education has been the habit of teaching the visual arts by historical and critical methods of appreciation and information instead of by participation in the processes and techniques of making things. Esthetic connoisseurship has generally displaced a creative conception of art.

Here, then, we find the very reason for the timid attitude so often shown when the architectural character of new college buildings has to be decided upon. We seem to have forgotten that there is an opportunity to make architectural history for ourselves and to have buildings designed in unmistakable terms of our own period.

What we need is a new code of visual values. So long as we flounder about in a limitless welter of borrowed artistic expression, we shall not succeed in giving form and substance to our own culture, for this implies selective choice of those artistic means which best express the ideas and spiritual directions of our time.

The impact of environment on a young man during his

college years is certainly decisive. If the college is to be the cultural breeding ground for the coming generation, its attitude should be creative, not imitative. Stimulating environment is just as important to free the student's creative talent as vigorous teaching.

Accordingly, the student needs the real thing, not buildings in disguise. So long as we do not ask him to go about in period clothes, it seems absurd to build college buildings in pseudo-period design. How can we expect our students to become bold and fearless in thought and action if we encase them timidly in sentimental shrines, feigning a culture which has long since disappeared?

The physical and spiritual functions determining the design of a building are interdependent. They are both part of our present life. It is an anachronism to express the physical functions with the newest technical means but to express the spiritual functions by borrowing a historical shell from the past. Such an attempt confuses the art of architecture with applied archeology. Genuine architecture of organic growth implies continuous renewal.

As history shows, the conception of "beauty" has changed along with progress in thought and technique. *Whenever man imagined he had found "eternal beauty," he fell back into imitation and stagnation. True tradition is the result of constant growth; its quality must be dynamic, not static, to serve as an inexhaustible stimulus to man.*

If, from this vantage point, I now look at my own immediate problem in hand—the design of the new Graduate Center for Harvard University—and contemplate the way in which these structures can be made into a vital link between the historic mission of a great educational institution and the restless, inquisitive minds of the young men and women of today, I know that it cannot be done without enlisting the student's wholehearted emotional response as well as by paying due respect to the specific architectural tradition of Harvard University.

What now is this tradition? Harvard's "Yard," so familiar to many sons of this country, shows a sound basic theme of architectural design which has been reverently kept throughout the centuries by almost all the architects who have contributed individual buildings; a composition of quadrangles, varying in size and confined by individually different buildings, offers a sequence of arresting surprises in space.

This spatial theme fulfills an ancient requirement of the art of architecture—namely, to balance artfully the building masses and open spaces in conformity with the human capacity to experience and sense harmonious space and scale.

The buildings themselves, however, though each is an integral part of the whole, do not "match." Harvard's most famous architectural bequests, built during three centuries, could hardly differ more strikingly in their enriching contrasts of forms and colors. Yet they all conform to the noble spatial pattern of the Harvard Yard.

Careful study of this existing pattern of open spaces and structures has therefore become the starting point for the design of the new Harvard Graduate Center. For here lies the inherent tradition of the Yard; its timeless pattern may well be interpreted again today in new terms of architecture, valid for present-day life.

There is no need to emulate the "atmosphere" of this or that period. *New buildings must be invented, not copied.* The great periods of architecture in the past have never imitated the periods of their forefathers. In one and the same famous building we can find, side by side, the characteristic shapes of the Romanesque, the Gothic and the Renaissance.

There is no copying to be found in order to preserve an external "cosmetic" uniformity. Unity was expressed by adherence to the given spatial order of existing buildings, not by imitating their veneers; exterior conformity was never mandatory in the past. Only our esthetic preoccupation with bygone periods has forced the "classical" façade on hundreds of college buildings built in the industrial age.

I believe that a different approach is needed which would seek to interpret by a new architectural expression the great changes which have taken place in our time.

For instance, it is a challenging problem in modern architecture to make use of repetitive standard parts, but at the same time to organize these parts in groups which vary in appearance. In the Graduate Center we strove to break the monotony which might have resulted from repetitive fenestration by changing the direction of the dormitory blocks as well as the design of their ends and links. This has resulted in a variety of different views for the onlooker.

We have also learned that the human being needs frequently changing impressions in order to keep his receptive abilities alert. *To produce such a stimulus for him contemporary artists and architects try to create the illusion of motion.* The confining, cagelike Georgian windows which in their time were necessary due to limitations in the manufacturing of glass have been supplanted by large window openings and undivided glass panes. These permit us to make sections of outdoor space a part of the total architectural composition which does not stop at walls as in the past, but produces the illusion of a continuity of space in motion. This new relationship of interior spaces to the infinite reaches of the outdoors is a characteristic new achievement of modern architecture which consciously or subconsciously must influence everybody's mind.

Building with elements of the handicraft periods in an age of industrialization is becoming more and more a hopeless task, which either bogs down in financial difficulties because of the paucity of skillful labor needed or ends in a lifeless fake product of industrial origin.

We cannot go on indefinitely reviving revivals. Architecture must move on or die. Its new life must come from the tremendous changes in the social and technical fields during the last two generations.

Neither medievalism nor colonialism can express the life of the twentieth-century man. *There is no finality in architecture —only continuous change.* VIP

7.

The Architect Within Our Industrial Society*

BACKGROUND Analysis. In my analysis I anticipate that architecture as an art starts beyond the demands of construction and economy on the psychological plane of human existence. *The satisfaction of the human psyche resulting from beauty is just as important for a full, civilized life, or even more so, than the fulfillment of our material comfort requirements.* The emotional blocks which bar the development of more organically balanced living must be met at the psychological level, just as our practical problems are met at the technical level.

Is the maker of the rose or the tulip an artist or a technician? Both, for *in nature utility and beauty are constitutional qualities, mutually and truthfully interdependent. The organic form process in nature is the perpetual model for every human creation, whether it results from the mental strife of the inventive scientist or from the intuition of the artist.*

We all still have before our mind that unity of environment and spirit that prevailed in the horse and buggy time. We sense that our own period has lost that unity, that the *sickness of*

* See: "Gropius Appraises Today's Architect," *Architectural Forum,* New York, May, 1952.

our present chaotic environment, its often pitiful ugliness and disorder have resulted from our failure to put basic human needs above economical and industrial requirements. Overwhelmed by the miraculous potentialities of the machine human greed has obviously interfered with the biological cycle of human companionship which keeps a community healthy. At the lower level of society the human being has been degraded by being used as an industrial tool. This is the real cause for the fight between capital and labor and for the deterioration of community relations. We now face the difficult task to rebalance the life of the community and to humanize the impact of the machine. It dawns on us that the social component weighs heavier than all the technical, economic and esthetic problems involved. *The key for a successful rebuilding of our environment—which is the architect's great task—will be our determination to let the human element be the dominant factor.*

But in spite of the effort of quite a few of us, we obviously did not yet find the spiritual bond to hold us together for a concerted effort at establishing a cultural denominator strong enough to becalm our fears and to grow into a common standard of expression.

The artists among us must grow impatient for such a synthesis, which would make whole what is now still unhappily disconnected.

We cannot deny that art and architecture had become an esthetic end in themselves, because they had lost touch with the community and the people during the industrial revolution. The external embellishments of a building were designed mainly to outdo those of the neighboring building instead of being developed as a type fit to be used repeatedly as a unit in an organic neighborhood pattern. The emphasis on being different instead of searching for a common denominator characterized our last generation of architects who dreaded the antihuman influence of the machine. The new philosophy in architecture recognizes the predominance of human and social requirements and it accepts the machine as the modern vehicle of form to fulfill these very requirements.

If we look backward into the past we discover the curious fact that a combination of both, a common denominator of form expression and individual variety was in evidence. *The desire to repeat a good standard form seems to be a function of society, and that was true long before the impact of industrialization.* The designation "standard" as such has nothing to do with the means of producing it—the hand tool or the machine. Our future houses will not necessarily be regimented because of standardization and prefabrication; natural competition on the free market will take care of individual variety of the component parts of buildings, just as we experience today a rich diversity of types for machine-made everyday goods on the market. Men did not hesitate to accept widely repeated, standard forms in the premachine periods of civilization. Such standards resulted from their means of production and from their way of living. They represented a combination of the very best many individuals have contributed to the solution of a problem. The standard forms of architecture of the past express a happy blend of technique and imagination, or rather a complete coincidence of both. This spirit—though by no means its dated forms— should be revived to create our own environment, with our new means of production, the machine.

But if they are not constantly checked and renewed, stand-

ards become stagnant. We know now that it is a futile attempt to try to match standards of the past, that our recent obsession with the idea that new buildings must always match existing ones betrayed a terrible weakness of our time, a silent admission of spiritual bankruptcy, for which there is no other example in the past. After the revolution in our own ranks, which has brought clarification, we seem to be set for a new creative effort. So it might be appropriate to investigate how far our professional framework fits the condition of our time, which I have tried to outline. Let's see whether the gigantic shift in the methods of production has been sufficiently recognized by us. For we have to see our case in the light of technological history and as we are not living in a period of sweet contemplation and security, we should reconsider our basic principles, for there are certainly some disturbing facts we cannot disregard any longer.

In the great periods of the past the architect was the "master of the crafts" or "master builder" who played a very prominent role within the whole production process of his time. But with the shift from crafts to industry he is no longer in this governing position.

Today the architect is not the "master of the building industry." Deserted by the best craftsmen (who have gone into industry, toolmaking, testing and researching), he has continued thinking in terms of the old craft methods, pathetically unaware of the colossal impact of industrialization. The architect is in a very real danger of losing his grip in competition with the engineer, the scientist and the builder unless he adjusts his attitude and aims to meet the new situation.

Separation of Design and Execution. Complete separation of design and execution of buildings, as it is in force today, seems to be altogether artificial if we compare it to the process of building in the great periods of the past. We have withdrawn much too far from that original and natural approach, when conception and realization of a building were one indivisible process and when architect and builder were one and the same person. *The architect of the future—if he wants to rise to the top again—will be forced by the trend of events to draw closer once more to the building production.* If he will build up a closely co-operating team together with the engineer, the scientist and the builder, then design, construction and economy may again become an entity—a fusion of art, science and business.

I will be more specific and reveal my target: The American Institute of Architects at its 1949 convention added to the mandatory rules of the Institute a new paragraph which reads: "An architect may not engage directly or indirectly in building contracting."

I have very great doubts about the wisdom of this rule which would perpetuate the separation of design and construction. Instead we should try to find an organic reunification which would return to us the mastery of the know-how in building. Of course, the intention of this mandatory paragraph has been a good one, namely to block unfair competition. But I am afraid that it represents merely a negative veto and does not try to solve our dilemma constructively.

Let us not deceive ourselves as to the strength of our present position in the eyes of our clients. The average private client seems to consider us as members of a luxury profession whom he can call in if there is some extra money available for "beautification." He does not seem to consider us as essential for the building effort as the builder and the engineer.

If you think I exaggerate, look at the facts in the U.S.A.:

More than 80 per cent of all U.S. buildings are being built without an architect.

Average income of the architect is less than a bricklayer makes in the East.

People generally do not understand the complicated task of the architect as we define it, and we have not been able sufficiently to clarify the issue.

When a client is in the building mood, he wants to buy the complete building for a fixed price and at a definite time of delivery. He is not at all interested in the question of the division of labor between architect, engineer and contractor. Since he senses subconsciously that it is rather artificial to keep design and building so wide apart, he usually concludes that the architect may be the unknown "X" in his calculations, in terms of money as well as time.

And what else can we expect? Are we not in an almost impossible position, having to meet a set price, though we have to start almost every commission with a kind of research and laboratory approach? Compare that with the long process in industry from paper design to test model to final product. In our field of design we have to absorb all the cost of research ourselves, for with us the model and the end product are one and the same. Has this not become an almost unsolvable task, particularly because it is subject to changes caused either by the client or by public agencies?

We often question the soundness of the business angle of our activities when we realize that the greater the ingenuity and the harder the work we devote to reducing costs, the more we are penalized by lesser payment. The client on the other hand assumes that it must be in the material interest of the architect to increase the building cost deliberately, since this would also increase the architect's percentage fee. So he often tries to settle for a lump sum fee. Of course we have to oppose that tendency of the client, as it is quite unfair to us, but that does not solve the ticklish problem in either direction. Here indeed is our greatest ethical dilemma. It often causes distrust on the part of the client, because of its inherent injustice to both parties; it even keeps many clients from seeking our service altogether.

Example of Industrial Designer. This does not happen to the designer of industrial products, who is usually paid for his initial service to develop the model, plus royalties from multiplication of the product. He benefits from the success of his work not only financially, but also in stature as a legitimate member of the team to which he belongs, along with the scientist, the engineer and the businessman. This process, developing more and more in industry, is carrying the previously isolated artist-designer back into the fold of society.

I am convinced that a similarly co-ordinated teamwork will also become the trend within the building industry. This should give the future architect, who is by vocation co-ordinator of the many activities concerned with building, once more the opportunity to become the master builder—if we are only willing to make the necessary changes in attitude and training. Of course, whether he shall be able, personally, to reach the high historical aim of his profession to integrate through his work all social, technical and esthetic components into a comprehensive, humanly appealing whole, that will depend on his creative vision. I say his "aim" for whether he actually *is* the master depends of course on his performance within the collaborating team. He cannot claim leadership as such, for the best man in a team should lead. *But the historical mission of the architect has always been to achieve the complete co-ordination of all efforts in building up man's physical surroundings.* If he wants to be faithful to this high mission, he must train the rising generation in conformity with the new means of industrial production instead of confining them to a training at the platonic drafting board, isolated from making and building.

Industrialization and Prefabrication. The machine certainly has not stopped at the threshold of building. The industrialization process of building seems only to take longer to complete than it took in other fields of production, since building is so much more complex. One component part of building after another is being taken out of the hands of the craftsman and given to the machine. We have only to look at manufacturers' catalogues to become convinced that already an infinite variety of industrialized component building parts exists at our disposal. In a gradual evolutionary procedure, the hand-building process of old is being transformed into an assembly process of ready-made industrial parts sent from the factory to the site. Furthermore, the proportionate percentage of mechanical equipment in our buildings is steadily increasing. Prefabrication has penetrated much further into the building of skyscrapers than into residential building.

But, to be honest with ourselves, we must admit that only relatively few of us architects have directly taken part in influencing and performing this great change, or in designing those component parts which we all use in building. It is the engineer and the scientist who have been instrumental in this development. That is why we have to speed up to regain lost ground by training our young generation of architects for their twofold task: (1) to join the building industry and to take active part in developing and forming all those component parts for building, and (2) to learn how to compose beautiful buildings from these industrialized parts. This presupposes, in my opinion, much more direct participation and experience in the workshop and in the field in contact with industry and builders than our usual training provides.

The coming generation of architects must bridge that fatal gap between design and building.

To begin with, let's stop squabbling about styles; every architect owes it to himself to defend the integrity of his design effort. What matters to the profession as a whole is to close ranks, to do some hard thinking together, and then to come to constructive decisions as to how we may reopen the gate leading into the field of building production for the benefit of the younger generation of architects. They are beginning to lose confidence in the trusteeship character of our professional setup and in its logical result: the self-appointed prima donna architect. *Architects in the future will refuse to be restrained from a natural urge to take actual part in a team effort with the industry to produce buildings and their parts. The emphasis, I believe, will be more and more on the team.*

Teamwork. For years I have been personally concerned, through my activities as an educator, with the plight of young architects as they leave school and enter into practice. I have seen them make valiant attempts to establish themselves independently, and I have seen them more often resign themselves to work indefinitely as draftsmen in large offices which offer little or no chance of exercising individual initiative. It is sad to see so much youthful energy and talent dry up by the slow attrition of our more and more centralized working system. Democratic concepts cannot easily survive the assaults of our increasing mechanization and superorganization, unless an antidote is used which may protect the individual in his struggle against the leveling effect of the mass mind.

I have tried to find such an antidote by introducing my students in Harvard, besides their individual training, to the experience of working in teams. This has become a valuable stimulant to students as well as to teachers who were all equally unacquainted with the advantages and difficulties of collaborating in groups. Now they had to learn to collaborate without losing their identity. This is to me an urgent task lying before the new generation, not only in the field of architecture but in all our endeavors to create an integrated society.

In our particular field there is no book of rules for such collaboration, unless we go back as far as the Middle Ages to study the working teams of the great cathedral builders. Most striking within the organization of those building guilds was the fact that until late in the eighteenth century every craftsman on the job was not an executing hand only, but was permitted to put his own design into his part of the work as long as he abided by the master's guiding key of design, which was the secret, geometrical auxiliary of the building guilds, similar to the keys in musical composition. Preconceived paper design hardly existed at all; the group lived together, discussed the task and built their ideas.

Compare this with our present conditions. We are expected to put all our design ideas, unto the last screw, into drawings and specifications. Then an army of workmen has to execute our design. We are hardly permitted to make any changes though there is no genius who could have sufficient foresight or imagination properly to judge the effect of every detail of his preconceived design; even less so the more he stays aloof from the practical process of building and making. Nor has the workman of today any chance to contribute to the design of a building. Since the time of the building guilds, collaboration among men, which would release the creative instincts of the individual instead of smothering them, has not been practiced much and we find very little knowledge about the basic requirements which made such teamwork possible. It is so unknown today in our profession that it is apt to be even viewed with apprehension, because the ideology of the past century has taught us to see in the individual genius the only embodiment of true and pure art. *It is true that the creative spark originates always with the individual, but by working in close collaboration with others toward a common aim, he will attain greater heights of achievement through the stimulation and challenging critique of his teammates, than by living in an ivory tower.* Of course, the creative mind asserts itself usually under any circumstance, even against heavy odds, but if we want to raise the average performance, teamwork becomes essential to sharpen and improve the individual contribution.

The *conditio sine qua non* of true teamwork is voluntariness; it cannot be established by command. It calls for an unprejudiced state of mind and for the firm belief that togetherness of thought and action is a prerequisite for the growth of human culture. Individual talent will assert itself quickly in such a group and will profit for its part from the cross-fertilization of minds in the give and take of daily contact. True leadership can emerge when all members have a chance to become leaders by performance, not by appointment. Leadership does not depend on innate talent only, but very much on one's intensity of conviction and devotion to serve. Serving and leading seem to be interdependent.

Our time is probably as rich as any in original talent, but too often this is doomed to spend itself in isolated accidental bursts of creativity because its message is lost for lack of a comprehensive response. If we could reclaim the individual genius for his natural task, i.e., to work as a *primus inter pares*—first among equals—instead of in exalted isolation, a much broader basis for understanding and response could be formed.

Certainly good intention alone is not sufficient for building up a team. We have to relearn methods of collaboration. It takes considerable time to acquire certain habits which seem indispensable for fruitful teamwork. I discovered that it was first of all imperative that every participant of the team must tell the other members right from the start what he is thinking and doing in a continuous mutual exchange. But even if everyone has the best intention to proceed that way in the beginning, it takes quite a while to train oneself to this end. Then this exchange becomes indispensable, as it places the different individuals in the right place within the collaborating team and, of course, everyone likes to do what he is particularly fitted for. Research then grows quickly, and a variety of opinions develops into a challenge for the team to come to final terms. In the flood of so many objective problems that have to be solved, the natural vanity of the individual is slowly drowned. The task grows gradually above the individual, who finally hardly remembers who initiated this or that part of the idea, as all their thoughts resulted from mutual stimulation. The stature of the individual grows under this voluntary collective effort of the team. As democracy obviously hinges on our ability to co-operate, I want the architect, as a co-ordinator by vocation, to lead the way toward developing the new technique of collaboration in teams. The essence of such technique should be to emphasize individual freedom of initiative, instead of authoritative direction by a boss. Experimenting with teamwork keeps one resilient and flexible and its methods are probably more adaptable to the rapid changes of our time than the boss-employee relationship. *Synchronizing all individual efforts the team can raise its integrated work to higher potentials than is represented by the sum of the work of just so many individuals.*

I should like to leave no doubt however that the type of team which will be effective for future building must certainly reach into the field of production. Increasing specialization needs ever growing co-ordination.

To accomplish the first of the twofold tasks of the future—the development of the component building parts—the architect needs to build up a team with the scientist and the manufacturer. His second task—the design of finished buildings from such component parts, and their actual assembly on the site—should be solved in a closely integrated collaboration between him, the engineer and the builder in direct contact with industrial methods and research.* It is quite obvious that we as individual architects have no facilities to test new materials and new technological methods, and even less to control our wealth of new technical potentialities the way the

* With this type of collaboration I do not refer to the so-called "package deal" corporations, as they treat architectural design more or less as a minor appendix only to the all-important business transaction. In the team which I have in mind the designer must have as much power of decision as the businessman and the builder. He must be a legitimate partner.

master builder of old controlled the crafts. In order to become more effective again for the whole process of building, we need the team and the production tools of industry. But we should not assume that our self-determined privilege to act as leader of the team will be accepted per se. As latecomers in industry we have to take the risk to join the team as equals and then to show by way of our own performance whether we shall be able to act as first among equals and so finally to change that rank order of public esteem in the architect's favor.

The essential difference of our industrialized society compared to a society of handcraftsmen rests upon the distribution of labor, not upon the tools used. A complicated textile machine represents only a refinement of the early hand loom. But it marks a change of principal importance if the entity of a working process is handled by one and the same craftsman, or if it is subdivided into many fragments, each of which is being put into the hands of another worker, as at the assembly line. It is this atomizing effect of the subdivision of labor which has exploded the coherence of the premachine society, not the machine itself. I confidently hope that organically built-up teamwork will gradually give us back that essential connectedness which is indispensable for a unity of effort.

I have merely tried to throw some light on the crossroad to which our profession has come. One of the two roads appears rough but wide and full of venture and hope. The other narrow one may lead into a dead end.

I have made my personal choice where to go, but being along in years, all I can do is to urge those who represent the next generation to search for a constructive solution how to correlate again design and execution in their future practice by direct participation in industrial and building production.

For I cannot convince myself that it shows a lack of integrity when a young architect and a young builder decide to join hands in order to build up a complete modern service—both design and building execution. We should instead actively encourage such a natural combination.

I have been asked whether it would not leave the client high and dry when he is deprived of the trustee control of his architect. My reply is that we do not need trustees for buying our everyday goods; we select them on account of the good reputation of the make or of the manufacturer. I do not see any difference as to buildings and their component parts. Of course, I know that the task of reconciling design and execution—which should be inseparable—will still meet a great many difficulties which can only be slowly solved in practice. But it is always a change of attitude first which precedes any implementation of a new course of direction.

This proposal I certainly do not think of as a cure-all for the ills that beset our profession. Nobody knows yet which measures will have to be taken to protect it against unfair competition, while at the same time giving the green light to those who want to take creative part also in the production itself of buildings and building parts. All I propose to do in today's state of fluidity is to keep the door open to a new set of problems, and knotty ones at that, which are the result of the impact of industrialization and must be solved by the new generation of architects.

8.

Architect — Servant or Leader?*

MODERN architecture is not a few branches of an old tree— it is new growth coming right from the roots. This does not mean, however, that we are witness to the sudden advent of a "new style." What we see and experience is a movement in flux which has created a fundamentally different outlook on architecture. Its underlying philosophy knits well with the big trends in today's science and art, steadying it against those forces which try to block its advance and to retard the growing power of its ideas.

What Constitutes a "Style"? The irrepressible urge of critics to classify contemporary movements which are still in flux by putting each neatly in a coffin with a style label on it has increased the widespread confusion in understanding the dynamic forces of the new movement in architecture and planning. What we looked for was a new approach not a new style. A style is a successive repetition of an expression which has become settled already as a common denominator for a whole period. *But the attempt to classify and thereby to freeze living art and architecture, while it is still in the formative stage, into a "style" or "ism" is more likely to stifle than*

* See: "Eight Steps toward a Solid Architecture" by W. Gropius, *Architectural Forum*, New York, February, 1954.

to stimulate creative activity. We live in a period of reshuffling our entire life; the old society went to pieces under the impact of the machine, the new one is still in the making. The flow of continuous growth, the change in expression in accordance with the changes of our life is what matters in our design work, not the hunt after formalistic "style" features.

And how deceiving a precipitate terminology can be! Let us analyze, for instance, that most unfortunate designation, "The International Style." It is not a style because it is still in flux, nor is it international because its tendency is the opposite—namely, to find regional, indigenous expression derived from the environment, the climate, the landscape, the habits of the people.

Styles in my opinion should be named and outlined by the historian only for past periods. In the present we lack the dispassionate attitude necessary for impersonal judgment of what is going on. As humans we are vain and jealous and that distorts objective vision. Why don't we leave it, then, to the future historians to settle the history of today's growth in architecture and go to work and let it grow? I'd like to suggest that in a period when the leading spirits of mankind try to see the human problems on earth as interdependent, as one world, any chauvinistic national prejudice regarding the shares claimed in the development of modern architecture must result in narrowing limitation. Why split hairs about who influenced whom when all that really matters is whether the results achieved improved our life? I dare say that we are all much more influenced by each other today than architects of former centuries because of the rapid development of interchange and intercommunication. This should be welcome as it enriches us and promotes a common denominator of understanding so badly needed. (I tried to encourage my students to let themselves be influenced by ideas of others, as long as they feel able to absorb and digest them and to give them new life in a context that represents their own approach to design.)

Search for Common Denominator Versus Ego Cult. If we look back to see what has been achieved during the last thirty or forty years we find that the artistic gentleman-architect who turned out charming Tudor mansions with all modern conveniences has almost vanished. This type of applied archeology is disappearing fast. *It is melting in the fire of our conviction that the architect should conceive buildings not as monuments but as receptacles for the flow of life which they have to serve, and that his conception must be flexible enough to create a background fit to absorb the dynamic features of our modern life.* We know that a period piece of architecture could never satisfy such a demand, but it is just as easy to create a modern straitjacket as a Tudor one—particularly if the architect approaches his task solely with the intention of creating a memorial to his own genius. This arrogant misapprehension of what a good architect should be often prevailed, even after the revolution against eclecticism had already set in. Designers who were searching for new expression in design would even outdo the eclecticist by striving to be "different," to seek the unique, the unheard of, the stunt.

This cult of the ego has delayed the general acceptance of the sound trends in modern architecture. Remnants of this mentality must be eliminated before the true spirit of the architectural revolution can take root among the people everywhere and produce a common form expression of our time after almost half a century of trial and error. *This will presuppose a determined attitude of the new architect to direct his efforts toward finding the type, the best common denominator instead of toward the provocative stunt.* Preconceived ideas of form, whether the outcome of personal whims or fashionable styles, tend to force the stream of life in a building into rigid channels and to hamper the natural activities of the people therein.

The pioneers of the new movement in architecture developed methodically a new approach to the whole problem of "design for living." Interested in relating their work to the life of the people, they tried to see the individual unit as part of a greater whole. This social idea contrasts strongly with the work of the egocentric prima donna architect who forces his personal fancy on an intimidated client, creating solitary monuments of individual esthetic significance.

The Client. By this statement I do not mean that we architects should docilely accept the client's views. We have to lead him into a conception which *we* must form to fit *his* needs. If he calls on us to fulfill some whims and fancies of his which do not make sense, we have to find out what real need may be behind these vague dreams of his and try to lead him in a consistent, over-all approach. We must spare no effort on our part to convince him conclusively and without conceit. We have to make the diagnosis of what the client needs on the strength of our competence. When a man is ill he certainly wouldn't insist on telling his physician how to treat him, but, if we expect such trust from our client, we learn that architects are rarely treated with the respect accorded to the medical profession. If we have not been competent enough to deserve being trusted, we had better make sure that we are in the future—in design, in construction and in economy, as well as in the social conception, which embraces the three other components of our work. If we neglect to make ourselves highly competent in all these fields, or if we shun responsibility in leading the way, we resign ourselves to the level of minor technicians.

Architecture needs conviction and leadership. It cannot be decided upon by clients or by Gallup Polls, which would most often only reveal a wish to continue what everybody knows best.

Machine and Science in Service of Human Life. There is another argument going on which, distorting the aims of modern architecture, needs clarification. We hear: "The modern accent is on living, not on the machine," and Le Corbusier's slogan, "The house is a machine for living," is old hat. With it goes a portrait of the early pioneers of the modern movement as men of rigid, mechanistic conceptions, addicted to the glorification of the machine and quite indifferent to intimate human values. Being one of these monsters myself, I wonder how we managed to survive on such meager fare. The truth is that the problem of how to humanize the machine was in the foreground of our early discussions and that a new way of living was the focus of our thoughts.

To devise new means to serve human ends, the Bauhaus, for instance, made an intense attempt to live what it preached and to find the balance in the struggle for utilitarian, esthetic and psychological demands. *Functionalism was not considered a rationalistic process merely. It embraced the psychological problems as well.* The idea was that our design should function both physically and psychologically. We realized that emotional needs are just as imperative as any utilitarian ones and demand to be satisfied. The machine and the new potentialities of science were of greatest interest to us, but the emphasis was not so much on the machine itself as on better use of the machine and science in the service of human life. Looking back, I find that our period has dealt too little with the machine, not too much.

What Is Regional Expression? Another confusing factor in the development of modern architecture is the appearance now and then of deserters from our cause who fall back on nineteenth-century eclecticism for lack of strength to go consistently through with a rejuvenation from the roots up. Designers turn back to features and fancies of the past to be mixed into the modern design, fondly believing that this will create greater popularity for modern architecture. They are too impatient to reach their goal by legitimate means and so they only conjure up a new "ism" instead of a new genuine regional expression. True regional character cannot be found through sentimental or imitative approach by incorporating either old emblems or the newest local fashions which disappear as fast as they appear. But if you take, for instance, the basic difference imposed on architectural design by the climatic conditions of California, say, as against Massachusetts, you will realize what diversity of expression can result from this fact alone if the architect will use the utterly contrasting indoor-outdoor relations of these two regions as focus for his design conception.

Here I should like to mention one problem that all architectural schools have in common: as long as our teaching centers only around the platonic drafting board we are perpetually in danger of raising the "precocious designer." For it is almost unavoidable that the lack of practical experience in the field, in the crafts and industrial processes of building leads at least some students to an all too ready acceptance of current style ideas, fads and clichés. This is the consequence of an all too academic training. Therefore, any opportunity to go into the field and to take part in all or any phases of the building process should be readily grasped by the young designer as a most essential discipline to establish balance between knowledge and experience.

Service and Leadership. But you might say, "What has this to do with the topic of this article: Architect—Servant or Leader?" The answer, already implicit in what I have said before, is simple: put an "and" in place of the "or." Serving and leading seem to be interdependent. The good architect must serve the people and simultaneously show real leadership built up upon a real conviction: leadership to guide his client as well as the working team entrusted with the job. Leadership does not depend on innate talent only, but very much also on one's intensity of conviction and willingness to serve. How can he reach this status? I have often been asked by students what I could advise them to do to become independent architects after leaving school and how they could avoid selling out their conviction to a society still pretty ignorant of the new ideas in architecture and planning.

My answer is this:

Making a living cannot be the only aim of a young man who should want above all to realize his own creative ideas. Your problem is, therefore, how to keep the integrity of your conviction intact, how to live what you preach, and still find your pay. You may not succeed in finding a position with an architect who shares your approach in design and who could give you further guidance. Then I would suggest you take a paying job wherever you can sell your skill, but keep your interests alive by a consistent effort carried on in leisure hours. Try to build up a working team with one or two friends in your neighborhood, choose a vital topic within your community, and try to solve it, step by step, in group work. Put ceaseless effort into it, then someday you will be able to offer the public, together with your group, a well-substantiated solution for this problem, for which you have become an expert. Meanwhile, publish it, exhibit it and you may succeed in becoming an adviser to your community authorities. Create strategic centers where people are confronted with a new reality and then try to weather the inevitable stage of violent criticism until people have learned to redevelop their atrophied physical and mental capacities to make the proper use of the proffered new setup. We have to discern between the vital, real needs of the people and the pattern of inertia and habit that is so often advanced as "the will of the people."

The stark and frightening realities of our world will not be softened by dressing them up with the "new look" and it will be equally futile to try to humanize our mechanized civilization by adding sentimental fripperies to our homes. *But if the human factor is becoming more and more dominant in our work, architecture will reveal the emotional qualities of the designer in the very bones of the buildings, not in the trimmings only; it will be the result of both good service and good leadership.*

III.

Planning and Housing

The sections under this chapter are mostly contributions I made to the CIAM—Congrés Internationaux d'Architecture Moderne—which is the most vital and consistent international organization aiming at "Total Architecture." The following statement was written for its twenty-fifth anniversary:

9.

CIAM 1928-1953*

DURING the twenty-five years of its existence I have been a devoted member of the CIAM. Now it seems fitting that I express myself as to what this international stronghold of architects and planners has meant to me during the long fight for a new architecture.

The most important was the fact that in a world full of confusion, of piecemeal efforts, a small, supranational group of architects felt the necessity to rally in an effort to see the many-sided problems that confronted them as a totality.

The decision to put this conception of totality above all limited objectives has determined our attitude, our convictions, our faith. It is this idea that acted like a magnetic force under the most diverse conditions and among groups of widely different national and racial traditions. It started in Europe, but today it reaches to the four corners of the earth. That has enriched us. The fact that the racial or national genius of different countries often tends to be preoccupied with one particular approach to our common adventure in living to the

---

* The CIAM—Congrés Internationaux d'Architecture Moderne—was established in 1928 in Château La Sarraz, Switzerland. The author has been one of its vice-presidents since 1929. For the aims and statutes of the CIAM see: *Can Our Cities Survive?* by J. L. Sert, Harvard University Press, 1942.

exclusion of others makes us feel how badly we need the corrective stimulus of other forms of living, emphasizing different values.

For instance: it seems that the youngest generation in the U.S.A.—down to the five-year-olds—is wholly fascinated by the problems of the conquest of outer space. They watch breathlessly as the scientists of the world are beginning to chart our way to the stars—even before we have succeeded in settling our earthly affairs. Their imagination is looking for new frontiers, almost unmindful of the confusion and derangement created during this ardent dash toward the unknown.

Brought face to face with the problems and blessings of those parts of the world that we call "the underdeveloped countries," we find their cultures have often given us a clearer insight into the deepest motives of human living than the complicated civilizations that we have created for ourselves. At this point we sometimes seem to regret the loss of their ancient roots and ties even more than they do themselves, but it would be a great mistake to think that they could preserve their integrity if they did not take part in the evolutionary process that binds us together now. The one thing they usually remember more distinctly than any of us is the fact that man lives also for the pursuit of happiness and I wish there would be more research by architects into what exactly are the prerequisites for this thing called "happiness." There was a time when architects were tempted to think that the possession of a nonleaking roof was the most important requirement for happiness, but we have since found out that though it may stop the rain, it does not necessarily create a happy human climate.

I want to affirm, therefore, that *I believe the creation of beauty and the forming of values and standards to be the innermost desire of a human being and that this moves him more deeply and more lastingly than the satisfactions of comfort. In our daily struggle to put that nonleaking roof over the heads of unsheltered millions we forget this too easily.*

CIAM, I confidently hope, will go on fighting for its original conception of totality with man as the measure for all our problems in planning and architecture.

10.

Sociological Premises for the Minimum Dwelling of Urban Industrial Populations*

THE over-all progress in housing design during the years following the First World War reveals that development of the minimum dwelling has reached a stalemate, evidently because deep-rooted changes in the social structure of nations which require the establishment of new standards in regard to the type and size of the necessary dwelling units have not received adequate attention. Determination of these changes in society must be the starting point for any work in this direction. Recognition of the evolutionary development of man's biological and sociological life processes must lead to a definition of the task at hand; only after this has been accomplished will it be possible to solve the second part of the problem, the establishment of a practical program for realizing the minimum dwelling.

The history of sociology is the story of man's gradual evolution from the wilderness through barbarism to civilization.

* See: "Die soziologischen Grundlagen der Minimalwohnung," *Die Justiz*, Vol. 5, No. 8 (1929), Verlag Dr. Walther Rothschild, Berlin-Grunewald.

The late German sociologist Müller-Lyer,* whose scientific results are referred to, distinguishes between four major legal eras of human society:

1. The era of kinship and tribal law
2. The era of the family and family law
3. The era of the individual and individual law
4. The future era of co-operatives and communal law

He establishes these as the successive phases of gradual social refinement. A detailed examination of these phases is useful because their regularity shows clearly that certain phenomena in modern society which are regarded by many as manifestations of regressive decay are actually evidence of evolutionary progress in a society which is in the process of stratification.

In prehistoric times the individual is only a member of society; his actions are purely social. The individual is not yet awakened.

The first signs of beginning individualism manifest themselves in the subjugation of woman by man. The patriarchal family arises and persists up to the formation of our modern industrial state.

The subjugation of woman is followed by the enslavement of man by the ruler. Stratification of society into lords and serfs liberates the ruling class so that it can devote itself to higher cultural problems. The masses are trained to labor, but the rights of the individual are suppressed.

Rule by force in the warring state is followed by rule by money in the industrial state. In both states the propertied class rules, the masses become impoverished. The industrial state, inspired by increasing scientific knowledge, develops more advanced methods of production. The exploitation of

* Dr. F. Müller-Lyer, *Die Entwicklungsstufen der Menschheit* [*Man's Phases of Development*], J. F. Lehmann, München, 1912.

nature offers the possibility of a life worthy of culture for all. Egotistical individualism gives way to social individualism. The fully developed individual becomes the aim of the state and the structure of society the means for its achievement.

Thus the concept of the tribe and the patriarchal family evolves into the ideal of an independent individual and finally into that of a future communal union which transcends the individual.

Inspired by the economic life of nations, the idea of rationalization is today growing into a major intellectual movement in which the actions of the individual are gradually being brought into beneficial relation with the welfare of society as a whole, a concept which transcends that of economic expediency for the individual alone. From the motive of "reason," social consciousness arises.

This evolutionary process is paralleled by changes in the structure and significance of the family.

The patriarchal family was characterized by supreme sovereignty of the family head. The wife lived in intellectual sterility and subjugation, and the children, even when grown up, were subordinated by absolute obedience to the will of the family head. Relatives and serfs, later the servants, apprentices and journeymen, were members of the larger family. The family was a self-sufficient microcosm, the unit of production and consumption in the state.

The eighteenth century marks the flight of serfs from the feudal master household to the free cities. The number of small families with their structure of parental sovereignty increases.

With the spread of the concept of the rights of the individual, the family progressively surrenders its functions to the state and thus the importance of the family unit in the sociological picture gradually decreases.

The invention of the machine leads to the socialization of labor. Goods are no longer produced for one's own needs but for the purpose of exchange within the society. One product of domestic industry after another is wrested from the family and transferred to socialized industry. The smaller unit, the family, thus loses its character as a self-contained productive unit.

With the progressive emergence of the individual the human birth rate decreases, in a manner analogous to phenomena observed in other forms of life, and it decreases in all civilized countries. The will of the individual, armed with the means provided by scientific achievements, tends toward voluntary birth control for reasons of predominantly economic nature. Within the span of one single generation the two-child pattern is established in all the civilized countries.

On the basis of surveys in the European countries and in America, the average family may be assumed to comprise 4.5 members. This number is averaged over urban as well as rural districts. The average family size in larger cities is below 4 throughout.

According to determinations by the German census bureau (1928), the birth rate in Germany was 35.6 per 1,000 population in the year 1900, and 18.4 per 1,000 population in the year 1927. It had thus decreased to a mere half. Nonetheless, there is still a birth excess of 6.4 per thousand.

In other civilized countries the decline in birth rate and the resulting decrease in family size progresses at a similar pace. The birth rate in the various countries decreases with increasing industrialization, but there is still an excess of births in them all.

In the patriarchal system the family alone was responsible for raising its children. Nowadays the state places a portion of the children's education in the hands of specially trained pedagogues in public schools. It thus intrudes into the relations between parents and children and regulates them according to the views of society. It establishes social security laws to provide insurance for old age, disease and physical handicap and thereby gradually relieves the family of its responsibility to care for the aged, the sick and the handicapped.

Whereas the sons in a patriarchal family inherited their father's trade, this caste system is dying out and the vocational castes which supersede the birth castes promote early departure from the parental home. The individual's mobility increases with the increasing transportation facilities, and the family is thereby diffused and diminished.

The patriarchal relationship between the family head and the journeymen, servants and apprentices is replaced by financial relationships as the barter economy is displaced by the financial economy. The activities of the family have become too limited to occupy all its members. The family domicile has become too expensive and too confined to shelter and employ the grown-up children permanently.

The former serfs become free servants, but with the progressive socialization of labor their number gradually decreases as more and more of them escape the family yoke to seek personal freedom and independence in industry. In most European countries today the demand for domestic servants exceeds the supply by a factor of two. In the United States the shortage of domestic help is already causing families to move into hotels, in which the domestic chores of the small family are economically centralized.

The confined dwelling is also losing its suitability for social intercourse, and intellectual inspiration is sought outside the family circle; the number of restaurants and clubs for men and women is increasing rapidly.

The rented apartment is replacing the ancestral family home, attachment to the home town ceases, and a new era of nomad individuals begins, fostered by the rapid development of mechanized transportation. The family is losing its home just as the tribe lost its territory. The cohesive power of the family is yielding to the rights of the individual citizen of the state. The conditions of socialized production enable the independent individual to change his place of employment at will, and population mobility is increasing tremendously. Most of the former family functions are gradually being assumed by society, and the importance of the family decreases despite its continued existence, while the state as such becomes institutionalized.

Past development thus shows steadily progressing socialization of former family functions of legal, pedagogic and domestic nature, and thus we perceive the first beginnings of a communal era which might someday displace the era of individual rights.

One further phenomenon has a decisive effect on the structure of the modern family. As the family era was ushered in by the rise of man, so the individual era is characterized by the awakening and progressive emancipation of woman. Woman's duty of obedience to man vanishes, and the laws of society gradually grant her rights equal to those of men. As the family transfers numerous domestic chores to the machinery of socialized production, woman's sphere of domestic activity shrinks and she looks beyond the family for an outlet for her natural need for occupation: she enters the world of business and industry. In turn industry, rejuvenated on basically new foundations by the machine, shows woman the impractical nature of her domestic hand labor.

Recognition of the shortcomings of the individual household awakens thoughts about new forms of centralized master households which partially relieve the individual woman of her domestic tasks by means of an improved centralized organization which is capable of performing them better and more economically than she can perform them herself, even when she applies all her efforts. The growing shortage of domestic help further emphasizes such desires. In the hard battle for subsistence faced by the entire family, the woman seeks ways of gaining free time for herself and her children while participating in gainful occupations and liberating herself from dependence upon the man. Thus the process does not seem to be motivated exclusively by the economic plight of urban populations, but it is the manifestation of an internal drive which is connected with the intellectual and economic emancipation of woman to equal partnership with man.

The organizational structure of such master households for single men and women, for children, widowed or divorced adults, for newlyweds or for ideological and economic communities of various forms is connected intimately with the problem of the minimum dwelling.

It is of course true that even in the present age, for which our practical work is intended, all forms of human society, old and new, continue to exist side by side; it is quite obvious, however, that one form predominates at any given time; the importance of the individual and his independent rights today overshadows that of the family as a sovereign unit. The rise to independence of the woman dissolved a powerful family bond; the forced marriage of old has practically vanished, and France in the days of the Revolution already considered marriage legally as merely a contract between citizens, which implies the right to divorce; woman finally achieved suffrage and thus political equality with man. Liberated from the limited horizon of the household, she extends her influence to cultural spheres.

The increasing independence achieved by woman produces modifications of a fundamental nature in the cornerstone of the family, the marriage contract. Originally a compulsory institution sanctioned by the state and the church, it evolves gradually into a voluntary union of persons who retain their intellectual and economic independence. Economically speaking, the family is reduced to the functions of reproduction and breeding selection. The stronger the organization of the social contract, the smaller the sphere remaining to the family. In its trend toward collective thinking, the institution of individualism is following the path pursued by its forerunner, the institution of family supremacy.

The evolutionary development outlined above is reflected by the following statistics, furnished by the German census bureau:

Divorces	1900	9,000
	1927	36,449
Illegitimate births	1900	8.7%
	1926	12.6%

In addition, according to information from physicians which it is difficult to obtain statistically, the number of abortions has increased substantially:

Individual households	1871	6.16%
	1910	7.26%
	1927	10.1 %

The ratio of the number of gainfully employed women to that of gainfully employed men (1920–21):

United States	1:4
Belgium	1:3
England and Sweden	2:5
Germany and Switzerland	1:2

According to information supplied by the Prussian district census bureau for Berlin in 1925:

Of 5 women above age 20, only 3 are married.
Of 3 gainfully employed persons, 2 are men and 1 is a woman.
Of 5 married women, 1 is gainfully employed.
Of 5 single women, 4 are gainfully employed.
Of 2 gainfully employed women, 1 is simultaneously a housewife.

In 1927 46% of all dwellings in Germany have only 1—3 rooms.

Policy-making government agencies charged with housing administration find it necessary, first of all, to observe the trends of social development, because the most difficult phase of their activity is the correct numerical estimation of the extent to which these general developments will progress within the population of their jurisdictional area. Only after formulation of this estimate are they in a position to distinguish between the numerical requirements for resolving both the older, familiar types of housing shortages, wherever they are still pronounced, as well as the newer, more individually differentiated needs, and to assign suitable housing to both groups. Almost all districts are still basing their policies of urban housing procurement to an excessive extent upon the old familial form of life, a pattern which by itself is no longer capable of describing the actual problems. It appears, instead, that the combination of a number of apartments in the form of a centralized master household has become necessary in order to lighten the burden of gainfully employed women and thus preserve them for marriage and reproduction.

The sociological facts must first be clarified in order that the ideal minimum of a life necessity, the dwelling, and the minimum cost of its production may be found; in view of the change in underlying principles, the program for a minimum dwelling can naturally not be solved by simply reducing the conventional, larger apartment in number of rooms and effective area. An entirely new formulation is required, based on a knowledge of the natural and sociological minimum requirements, unobscured by the veil of traditionally imagined historical needs. We must attempt to establish minimum standards for all countries, based on biological facts and geographic and climatic conditions. This approach is in the spirit of the impending equalization of life requirements under the influence of travel and world trade.

The problem of the minimum dwelling is that of establishing the elementary minimum of space, air, light and heat required by man in order that he be able to fully develop his life functions without experiencing restrictions due to his dwelling, i.e., a minimum *modus vivendi* in place of a *modus non moriendi*. The actual minimum varies according to local conditions of city and country, landscape and climate; a given quantity of air space in the dwelling has different meanings in a narrow city street and in a sparsely settled suburb. Von Drigalski, Paul Vogler and other hygienists observe that, given good conditions of ventilation and sunlight, man's requirements of living space from the biological viewpoint are very small, particularly if the space is correctly organized for efficiency; a graphic picture of the superiority of a small modern apartment over an obsolete one is provided by the comparison offered by a well-known architect between an ingeniously arranged wardrobe trunk and a crate.

However, if the provision of light, sun, air and warmth is culturally more important and, with normal land prices, more economical than an increase in space, then the rules dictate: enlarge the windows, reduce the size of rooms, economize on food rather than heat. Just as it was formerly customary to overestimate the value of food calories in comparison with that of vitamins, many people nowadays erroneously regard larger rooms and larger apartments as the desirable aim in dwelling design.

To allow for the increasing development of more pronounced individuality of life within the society and the individual's justified demand for occasional withdrawal from his surroundings, it is necessary, moreover, to establish the following ideal minimum requirement: *every adult shall have his own room, small though it may be!* The basic dwelling implied by these fundamental requirements would then represent the practical minimum which fulfills its purpose and intentions: the standard dwelling.

The same biological considerations which determine the size of the minimum dwelling are also determinative in regard to its grouping and incorporation into the city plan. *Maximum light, sun and air for all dwellings!* In view of differences in the quality of the air and the intensity of the light, an attempt must be made to establish a numerically defined lower limit, on the basis of which the required amount of light and air can be calculated for given local conditions. General quantitative regulations which fail to allow for differences, as they exist at present, are useless in many cases. To be sure, it is the basic aim of all urban building codes to ensure light and air for dwellings. Every new building code has surpassed its predecessor in striving to decrease the population density and thereby to improve conditions of light and air. However, all means employed thus far for decreasing population density are based on the concept of the permanent, close-knit family. The only ideal solution was thought to be the single detached dwelling, the one-family house with garden, and on the basis of this aim the excessive population density of cities was combatted by limiting building height. However, this aim is no longer adequate today, as sociology shows, because it satisfies only a portion of the public needs, but not the needs of the industrial population, which is the primary object of our investigations. The internal structure of the industrial family makes it turn from the one-family house toward the multistory apartment house, and finally toward the centralized master household. The healthy tendency to progressively decrease the population density in cities is in no way endangered by this new form of dwelling, since the population density of a zone can be controlled without limiting the building height by merely establishing a quantitative ratio of dwelling area or building volume to building lot area. This would pave the way for a vertical development of the multistory apartment building. Whereas the detached one-family house is more suited to the needs of other, wealthier population classes which are not under consideration at present, the large apartment building satisfies more nearly the sociological requirements of present-day industrial populations with their symptomatic liberation of the individual and early separation of the children from the family. In addition, the large high-rise apartment building offers considerable cultural advantages as compared to the walk-up apartment house with a small number of floors. For a comparison in the case of alternating parallel blocks of apartments with north-south orientation and having blocks of varying height (two to ten floors), see Fig. 40, a, b, c, d.

The results derived from this comparison ensure that the large high-rise apartment building will have the biologically important advantages of more sun and light, larger distances between neighboring buildings, and the possibility of providing extensive, connected parks and play areas between the blocks. It thus appears necessary to develop the well-organized high-rise apartment building technically, incorporating in its design the ideas of the centralized master household, i.e., to develop gradually the centralization and specialization of the domestic work associated with the small family. Such a large apartment house does not represent a necessary evil accompanying a period of regressive decay, but a biologically motivated, genuine residential building type of the future for urban industrial populations.

The objections of one-sided defenders of houses against the idea of the residential skyscraper on the grounds that natural instincts attach man to the ground are without biological foundation.

Modern urban industrial population is derived directly from the rural population. It retains its primitive standard of living, which frequently even decreases, instead of developing expanded requirements corresponding to its new way of life. The attempt to adapt its housing requirements to its old form of life appears regressive for the reasons described and altogether incompatible with its new form of life.

Previous experience in the various countries reveals that there is a gap between the cost of producing dwellings and the average income of the families. It is thus not possible to satisfy the housing requirements of the masses within the framework of a free economy. As a result, the state is beginning to relieve the family provider of a portion of his responsibilities in this respect as well and to gradually equalize the discrepancies caused by present rent levels with the aid of subsidies and other measures. Indeed, the construction of low-cost dwellings offers little temptation to industry and banking, whose natural tendency it is to derive maximum profits from production and investments. Since technology operates within the framework of industry and finance and since any cost reduction achieved must first of all be exploited for the benefit of private industry, it will only be able to provide cheaper and more varied dwellings if the government increases private industry's interest in dwelling construction by increased welfare measures. If the minimum dwelling is to be realized at rent levels which the population can afford, the government must therefore be requested to:

1. Prevent the waste of public funds for apartments of excessive size, while facilitating the financing of the construction of minimum dwellings, for which an upper limit of apartment size must be established.

2. Reduce the initial cost of roads and utilities.

3. Provide the building sites and remove them from the hands of speculators.

4. Liberalize as far as possible the zoning regulations and building codes.

On the average, one-quarter of the income is considered a tolerable rent. It will have to be determined whether or not the program to be planned can be realized within the scope of actual rent levels.

However, present-day minimum requirements of apartment hunters, which are a result of impoverishment, should not serve as a criterion for establishing the minimum dwelling if an absolute, biologically motivated result is to be achieved; it would therefore also be incorrect to base the program on the present income of the average family. Instead, the properly established standard, the "rationed dwelling," must become the minimum requirement of every gainfully employed person; it then is up to the community to find means for making this "rationed dwelling" accessible to all the employed.

II.

Houses, Walk-ups or High-rise
Apartment Blocks?*

WHAT is the most rational building height in the grouping of low-cost dwellings from the viewpoint of city planning? To clarify the problem, it seems expedient to first define more closely the concept "rational." The term literally means "according to reason," and thus in the present case it implies not only economic considerations, but primarily also those of psychological and sociological nature. The sociological aspects of a wholesome housing policy are unquestionably of more vital importance than the purely economic aspects, because economics for all its importance is not an end in itself but only a means to an end. Rationalization therefore makes sense only if it tends to enrich life or, in the language of economics, if it spares the most precious of commodities, the vitality of the people.

Currently valid opinions concerning building heights to be considered expedient in urban dwelling construction are characterized by the following sentences from the German

* See: CIAM, *Rationelle Bebauungsweisen,* "Flach—Mittel—oder Hochbau?" by Walter Gropius, pp. 26–47, Verlag Englert & Schlosser, 1931. "Das Wohnhochhaus" by W. Gropius, *Das Neue Frankfurt,* February 1931, Internationale Monatsschrift, Frankfurt/M.

Government Directives for the Housing Industry for the year 1929:

> The dwellings must be provided in buildings which satisfy modern health requirements, particularly in regard to adequate illumination and ventilation. These requirements are best satisfied by small house construction in the wider sense of the word. The aim should be one-family dwellings with gardens. If local conditions require large apartment houses, the height of such buildings is to be limited to a maximum of three residential stories in medium-size towns and to a maximum of four residential stories in larger cities. Only in special cases in several metropolitan cities should these heights be exceeded, and even in these cases a decrease in building heights by zoning laws should be strived for, particularly in outlying districts.

The attitude reflected by these words, which is probably paralleled to a somewhat less pronounced extent in the majority of other countries, was initially inspired by the sound intention to reduce the population density in cities which in many cases has become excessive, mainly due to real estate speculation. It is up to the government to act in the general interest in remedying the tragic situation in which the very land we live on is subjected to the market manipulations of the business world.

The ravages following wild building activity in the cities brought about the healthy reaction of a back-to-nature trend and a battle of authorities and private citizens to settle the majority of the population in one-family houses with gardens. This form of dwelling is undoubtedly excellent in many respects, and public measures to promote single dwelling construction are to be welcomed. It is a fallacy, on the other hand, to apply the natural tendency toward height limitation in house construction to the multifamily dwelling as well, because the aim of reducing population density can be achieved by more rational procedures than the usual "down-zoning." Suggestions in regard to this important problem will follow later. Economic experience gained during the past years and readjustments in the living and dwelling habits of many social classes leave no doubt that the one-sided efforts in favor of individual home production resulted in a neglect of apartment house construction and led to confusion which had a detrimental effect on the entire housing policy. According to the present state of affairs, the tendency to house the majority of the population in detached dwellings is undoubtedly an economic utopia. But is this aim at all justified? Is the one-family house with a garden borrowed from country life in every respect the ideal solution for the urban industrial population which longs for nature? Does this type of housing in itself ensure the full physical and spiritual development of its occupants? Is a reasonable development of the city conceivable if all its citizens live in single homes with gardens? I do not think so. But let us examine the basic premises of the problem in order that we may define the optimum limits between houses and high-rise apartment blocks.

Premises. Violently conflicting opinions concerning the ideal type of housing persist: the root of the controversy is the old antithesis of city versus country. Man requires contrasts for stimulation and relaxation, and the urbanite's longing for the country as well as the country dweller's longing for the city are elementary drives constantly in need of satisfaction. Progressing development ameliorates the sharp contrast by bringing the comforts of the city to the country and returning the charms of nature to the city. The less this double drive is satisfied (and this frustration is more or less prevalent, particularly in large cities), the more violent the battle for equalizing factors, such as the house in a garden. The battle for the ideal type of housing is psychological in its origin and consequently subject to panicky reversals and psychoses such as the one we observed in the passionate fight against the tenements.

The essentials for wholesome life are, in addition to adequate food and warmth: light, air and elbow room. Undoubtedly these three cardinal conditions for a livable dwelling are more completely satisfied by the one-family house than by the tabooed cold water flats in crowded tenement sections. However, the cause for the misery of these undignified dwellings is not the dwelling form of the multistory apartment house as such but the shortsighted legislation which permitted the construction of this class of low-cost dwellings to fall into the hands of unscrupulous speculators without adequate social safeguards. Responsibly planned high-rise apartment blocks situated on wide expanses of green with ample space between them are certainly capable of satisfying all the requirements of light, air and elbow room while simultaneously offering the urbanite a wealth of other advantages.

The special character of metropolitan housing developments for settling large numbers of working people around a concentrated city core makes for short commuting distances, which implies the use of multistory construction to reduce horizontal distances. The single-family house is contradictory to this basic trend of the city. It is the task of the city planner not merely to improve transportation facilities, but rather to reduce the need for them. The citizens of Los Angeles, by

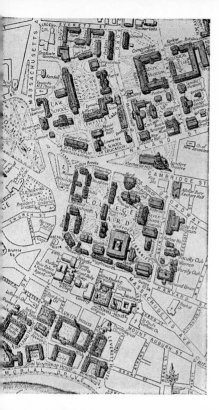

Fig. 36: The Harvard Yard. The new Graduate Center is on top

Fig. 37: The Harvard Graduate Center (Architect—the Architects Collaborative, 1949). Photo—Fred Stone, Cambridge

Fig. 38: Church in Bergamo, Italy, showing side by side Romanesque, Gothic and Renaissance building elements. Photo—Konrad Wachsmann

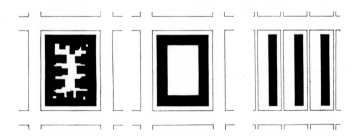

Fig. 39: Comparison of old and new methods of block division

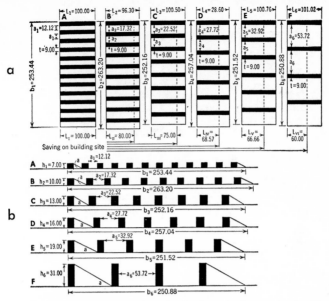

Fig. 40 a, b, c, d: Diagram showing the development of a rectangular site with parallel rows of apartment blocks of different heights. Conditions as to air, sun, view and distance from neighbor block are improved with increased height of the blocks in c and d. In a and b these conditions are constant, but the higher the buildings the less land is needed for the same amount of living space.

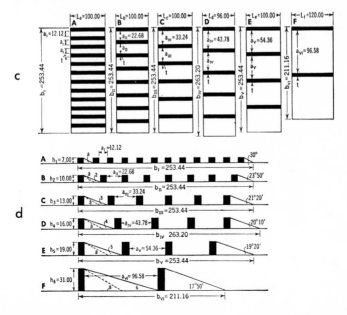

Fig. 41: Plaza San Marco, Venice

Fig. 42:

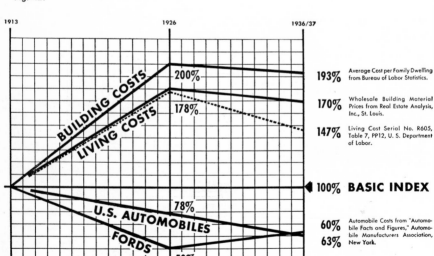

1913 1926 1936/37

193% Average Cost per Family Dwelling from Bureau of Labor Statistics.

170% Wholesale Building Material Prices from Real Estate Analysis, Inc., St. Louis.

147% Living Cost Serial No. R605, Table 7, PP12, U. S. Department of Labor.

◀ **100% BASIC INDEX**

60% Automobile Costs from "Automobile Facts and Figures," Automobile Manufacturers Association, New York.
63%

200%

178%

BUILDING COSTS

LIVING COSTS

78%

U.S. AUTOMOBILES

FORDS

50%

Fig. 43: A New York street—a riot of styles, forms and colors

Fig. 44a: Peter Breughel, a village square. Streets and squares here are still fitting receptacles for social intercourse of the whole community

Fig. 44b: But what has happened now to the pedestrian?

COPY

area the largest city of the world and consisting almost exclusively of single homes, spend a large fraction of each day commuting to and from their places of work or business; their sacrifice of time and money for daily travel is many times that of the German working population, whose average commuting distance is long enough as it is. The director of the research institute for hygiene and immunization of the Kaiser-Wilhelm Institute in Berlin Dahlem, Professor Friedberger, calculates the average commuting expenses of a gainfully employed family of four in Berlin which is forced to live in the suburbs while working in the city to be 139 per cent of a typical peacetime rent; in twenty-five years and assuming an interest rate of only 3.5 per cent, this commuting cost adds up to an amount equal to twice the cost of building an inexpensive dwelling. Assuming a commuting trip of only half an hour to and from work, he finds that the 2,200,000 working people in Berlin spend a total of 37,500,000 eight-hour working days each year commuting; each individual loses two working years during an average working life of thirty years. Imagine what the corresponding figures for Los Angeles would be!

Thus for the average low-income population, suburban life is uneconomical. To quote Friedberger's conclusion from his investigations:

High-rise buildings surrounded by as much landscaping as possible thus appear to be the only housing type suitable for metropolitan areas. The sins of a fallacious housing policy and particularly of incorrect land use during the growth period of our metropolitan cities have virtually brought the only type of housing appropriate for large cities into disrepute. The natural reaction to the justly despised, improperly executed and exploited "tenement" inspired a general desire for individual homes, the migration toward the suburbs of metropolitan cities. The movement was not based as much on rational considerations as on wishful thinking tinged by emotional bias. Unfortunately the iron laws of economics do not yield to wishful housing policies. Public welfare standards which are too highly aimed are actually injurious to the public insofar as they make it impossible to provide that which is actually economically feasible for the largest possible number of people.

Sober economic considerations are too easily overshadowed by the dream of a single home.

Friedberger's verdict carries all the more weight, coming from a responsible hygienist.

The opponents of urban apartment houses ascribe decreases in the birth rate and the spread of diseases to the crowded living conditions in large cities, an accusation which certainly seems plausible on the surface. But strangely enough, certain important facts contradict this assumption. Although according to the volume for 1928 of the *Statistical Report on Germany* the over-all birth rate for the entire country is 18.6 per thousand population, while the figure for all large cities is only 13.6, the rate averaged over the Western industrial regions of particularly high population density is 20 per thousand and thus exceeds the over-all average for the entire country. Von Drigalski, city health official in Berlin, and Krautwig, hygienist in Cologne, observe that the spread of communicable diseases is in no way connected with crowded living conditions and the small size of dwellings, but with the inadequate illumination and ventilation of substandard apartments which, in addition, are occupied by undernourished low-income groups.

In his "Investigation Concerning Living Conditions, Particularly in Small Apartments," Friedberger debunks the dogma that the worst living conditions are found in large cities. Simultaneously, on the basis of research by others (Karl Flügge) as well as his own careful investigation of urban and rural living conditions he arrives at the conclusion that theories concerning impairment of health due to living conditions, particularly in large cities, have suffered severely.

If we can rely on these pronouncements it follows that *apartment houses are above reproach from the health viewpoint, providing of course that good conditions of illumination and ventilation are provided. The two extreme types of housing, low and high, are thus not inherently good or bad, but their different characteristics require different applications.* Let us compare:

The occupant of an individual home buys the advantages of more quiet and outdoor life in sparsely settled residential districts in exchange for the disadvantages of long commuting distances, loss of spare time in crowded public conveyances with danger of infection, long distances to school for the children and more difficult shopping. The occupant of an apartment house, on the other hand, must pay for the time gained due to decreased horizontal distances with the loss of direct access to the outdoors and the necessity of using stairs or elevators. The single home with a garden is more suitable for families with children in higher-income brackets who are permanently settled and do not depend on changes in place of employment and on repeated moving, while the rented dwelling in an apartment house is better adapted to the needs of the more mobile working class. The one-family house fails to meet the needs, in regard to cost or otherwise, of this largest group of housing consumers because its universal introduction is prohibited, not by the ravages of a capitalistic society, but by the very nature of cities. Dr. Martin Wagner, former building commissioner of Berlin, a passionate defender of house construction, considers it an established fact that the one-family house is not feasible as a minimum dwelling but only for larger families, and that, moreover, its initial cost and site requirements are greater than in the case of an apartment home of equal size. These facts are inescapable, and therefore the one-family house will remain reserved for a higher stratum of the population. However, since it undoubtedly offers many valuable contributions to family life, particularly with a view to children, the government must promote the distribution and construction of this type of housing wherever the need for single homes exists, even if the economic difficulties involved are greater than in the case of apartment house construction. In choosing a type of housing one should not only compare the cost of construction, but also the cost of maintenance in time and money. The latter item in particular is larger in the case of the one-family house, especially if commuting costs are included. In particular, also, low-income families lack the time required to care for a house and garden if they are not to deteriorate.

There is an undeniable need to liberate the overworked housewife in the average urban low-income family by labor-saving devices in the home so that she will have free time for herself and her children and be able to contribute to the family income. It should also be borne in mind that modern woman is seeking relief from housework in order to participate in the gainful activities of the family not merely out of financial necessity, but to satisfy her innate drive for increasing independence. Far more effective relief is provided by the apartment than by the individual home, particularly if the former provides centralized servicing facilities. In a poll of the Reich's league of housewives, 60 per cent declared themselves in favor of apartment house dwellings. The verdict of practicing social workers indicates that on the basis of their experience they consider single homes suitable only for the highest-income bracket of the working class, while the apartment house is the only reasonable housing type for the bulk of the lower-income groups.

Experience gained in the field of housing construction with due consideration of factors other than purely economic ones has shown that the construction of individual homes cannot be expected to provide for the bulk of the working population; that, indeed, this type of housing is often actually opposed by them. It follows that well-organized, modern high-rise apartment blocks cannot be considered a necessary evil; they are a biologically motivated type of dwelling, a genuine by-product of our age. The objections of one-sided defenders of one-family house construction on the grounds that the nature of man roots him to the soil (an assertion entirely lacking scientific proof) is in direct conflict with the intuitive preference of many persons who feel particularly at home in an elevated apartment because they prefer the greater peace in upper stories (no noise from street or playgrounds) and the unobstructed view.

Building Heights.   What then is the optimum height of apartment houses, three, four, five, ten or fifty stories?

I share the view that it is sentimental self-deceit to assert that a fourth-floor apartment without elevator is in more intimate contact with "nature" than one on the tenth floor; it is very questionable whether the owner of an individual house with his intimate contact with the noise, odors and dust on the ground will live more quietly or healthfully than his considerably poorer colleague on the tenth floor of a soundly planned and well-equipped high-rise development. In my opinion the optimum height of an apartment house is a purely economic problem whose solution has unfortunately not yet been clarified in all respects due to lack of practical experiments.

The systematic cultivation of high-rise apartment block design and improvement of the codes, for example in regard to elevators and installations, will increase the relative construction cost with increasing number of floors, particularly due to the increasing numbers of elevators required, but the costs of streets and public utilities will decrease simultaneously. The limits of economic expediency are defined by the height beyond which the increase in construction cost is no longer compensated by savings in site and road requirements. The most economic building height will be found at this point; it depends upon the cost of land in each particular case.

Land Use. This leads me to the question of land use, which I shall discuss on the basis of conditions in Germany. What is the prevailing situation?

Every building code thus far has surpassed its predecessor in the attempt to improve health conditions for the inhabitants of densely populated sections, but even the newest codes bear the stamp of a fight between speculation and public authority instead of applying systematic curbs to private interests based on a farsighted, social idea rooted in the proper biological premises for wholesome dwelling conditions. Even present building codes fail to provide adequate possibilities of bringing nature to the doorstep of the residents of sections with high-density zoning. The terrible light-well apartments of the late nineteenth century were eliminated by unified postwar building codes; they were replaced by city block units of peripheral buildings surrounding an interior courtyard, the customary method of today. But this type of construction still has the great disadvantage of inadequate illumination and ventilation. The practice of surrounding the city block entirely on all sides results in unfavorable orientation with inevitable northern exposures for a large number of the apartments, as well as unsatisfactory corner solutions, with overshadowed apartments; important health requirements are thus ignored. This building code is in need of revision; particularly, however, the zoning laws. These legal changes will be dominated by emphasis on parallel instead of peripheral apartment blocks. This grouping provides considerable advantages for the site and has recently been used to an ever increasing extent. Parallel rows of apartment blocks have the great advantage over the old peripheral blocks that all apartments can have equally favorable orientation with respect to the sun, that the ventilation of blocks is not obstructed by transverse blocks, and that the stifled corner apartments are eliminated. Such parallel rows also provide for systematic separation of highways, residential streets and footwalks more easily and at less cost than in the case of peripheral construction. It makes for better illumination and more quiet, and also decreases the cost of road building and utilities without decreasing the effectiveness of land use. The over-all distribution is thus considerably functionalized, resulting in improved conditions of hygiene, economy and traffic.*

* Compared to the first, rather rigid, experiments in the field of a new distribution for urban dwellings, we have progressed today to a much

These advantages could be further increased considerably if new legislation would impose limitations on population density instead of building heights, i.e., if it controlled the quantitative ratio of dwelling area or building volume to site area. Comparative studies I made reveal that *hygienic and economic conditions become more favorable in many respects as the number of stories increases, and that high-rise apartment blocks are thus superior to the conventional walk-ups of three, four or five floors with inadequate park strips between blocks and insufficient distances between window fronts.* In my comparisons I assume that both fronts of the parallel apartment blocks are to have at least two hours of sunlight on December 21, when the sun is at its lowest.

According to Heiligenthal, this leads to the rule of thumb that the distance between parallel blocks must be one and one half times the building height in the case of blocks oriented in the north-south direction, two and one half times the building height in the case of east-west orientation, and twice the building height in the case of diagonal orientation. This rule shows that north-south orientation is the most favorable in regard to efficiency of land use. Moreover, the majority of dwelling plans in Northern Europe are best suited to an east-west exposure of their two fronts. On the basis of these facts I made a comparative study of parallel blocks with north-south orientation having alternatively from two to ten stories built on a given site, and I deduced the following rules, which will serve to support my suggestions for amending the regulations concerning population density (see Fig. 40, a, b, c, d) :

---

more unorthodox and varied grouping of apartment blocks. The prevalent opinion is that the optimum of orientation has to be compromised sometimes to avoid dull regularity at all costs.

1. *Assuming a site of given size and a given angle of sunlight incidence* (30°), *i.e., a given illumination condition, the number of beds increases with the number of stories.*

2. *Assuming a given angle of sunlight incidence and distributing a given number of beds* (15 *square meters or* 161 *square feet of area per bed*) *into parallel apartment blocks with varying number of stories, the size of the required site decreases with increasing number of stories.*

3. *Assuming a building site of given size and a given number of beds and varying the number of stories, the angle of sunlight incidence decreases with increasing number of floors, i.e., the conditions of illumination improve with increased height.*

For a given utilization of the site and a given dwelling area or number of beds, the distance between apartment blocks in the case of a ten-story building has increased to almost twice the minimum distance prescribed by the rule of thumb, and that without any economic sacrifice. This is a striking gain. It is thus absurd that current legislation imposes limits on building height instead of dwelling area or building volume, which deprives the public of these obvious economic and hygienic advantages. In a ten- or twelve-story high-rise apartment block even the ground floor occupant can see the sky. Instead of lawn strips only 20 meters (66 feet) wide, the windows face landscaped areas with trees which are 100 meters (328 feet) wide and help to purify the air as well as providing playgrounds for the children. Here nature penetrates the city and offers the urbanite new charms; and if all roof areas were made into gardens, which has rarely been done, then the city dweller will have succeeded in reconquering the land which is lost on the ground when the house is built. *The large city must assert itself; it requires a development of its own, a type of dwelling adapted to its own life which provides a maximum of air, sunlight and vegetation with a minimum of traffic and maintenance needs.* The high-rise apartment block is capable of fulfilling these requirements, and therefore its promotion is among the most pressing tasks of the housing policy.

Advantages and Disadvantages of High-rise Apartment Blocks. One fear remains: the lack of a direct connection between the dwelling and the ground. The safety of elevators must be increased sufficiently so that children can use them without danger, and this is an economic rather than a technical problem. Prejudice against high-rise buildings is frequently ascribed to the difficulty of supervising children. The kindergartens of today are still no cure for this situation. Nevertheless, the well-managed, hygienically improved kindergarten (most expediently located in the landscaped areas between the parallel blocks) and the nursery for babies (located in the roof gardens) should be the proper solution. The children themselves frequently oppose group organization, but it must be remembered that schools and hospitals once met with the same opposition. However, the socialization of the urban family is progressing irrevocably, and the democratic nature of the high-rise apartment building and of the centrally serviced household corresponds to this trend. The individual's need for seclusion, which frequently enters the argument against high-rise buildings, should not be overestimated. It is best satisfied by fulfillment of the requirement that each adult shall have his own room, small though it may be, to which he can retire. Very much is made of mutual co-operation among families, which is of course much more readily possible in a high-rise apartment building than in an individual home. And only high-rise apartment blocks can relieve the individual occupant of a large fraction of the most tedious and time-consuming domestic chores by means of its centralized service installations; these are also of importance from the viewpoint of national economy because of their over-all savings in material and time. Is it of no importance that the overburdened housewife in the modern industrial worker's family no longer needs to carry the coal upstairs and tend to the furnace for heat and hot water? That the service center handles her laundry more efficiently then she could herself? That the advent of electric refrigerators, vacuum cleaners, mechanical ventilators, centralized kitchen installations, and finally even communal recreation rooms, sport facilities and kindergartens is approaching? The cost of such conveniences can be distributed economically over a large number of families in a high-rise apartment block, costs whose purpose it is to transform saved time into the most valuable commodity of all: creative leisure!

I believe that the idea of high-rise apartment blocks has now been clarified and its indispensability for modern cities proven, but habits cannot be conquered by reason alone, because intellectual adaptation is not enough; only practice can conquer the prevailing mentality, and we must fight in all countries in favor of the construction of high-rise apartment blocks. The first high-rise developments should be built for younger, more favorably situated families who will show a desire to test and help develop this new way of life and living. The entire housing industry will then inevitably become convinced that only high-rise apartment blocks can assure the urban population of a maximum in living comfort in regard to health and transportation at a price it can afford.

To sum up:

The city dweller's choice of the type of his dwelling must be aimed at achieving the maximum value within his reach. This choice depends upon his inclinations, his occupation and his budget.

The dwelling in a house with garden offers more quiet, more seclusion, more recreation facilities and elbow room in one's own garden, and greater ease in the supervision of children; it is not economical as a minimum dwelling, its maintenance is more expensive and time-consuming, it makes for long commuting distances and ties down its occupants.

The dwelling in an apartment house ensures short commuting distances and provides economical centralized services for housekeeping and recreation; it causes some difficulties in the supervision of children outdoors due to the vertical distances from the ground, but it is economical as a minimum dwelling and promotes community spirit.

Walk-up apartment buildings have the disadvantage of inadequate distances between them, of insufficient sunlight, narrow park strips and inadequate outdoor space. The high-rise apartment block, on the other hand, is much airier, sunnier and more separated, it provides a maximum of wide park areas in which, above all, children can satisfy their need for play and noise. It is also more favorable in regard to the cost distribution of central services.

Its advantages are decisive for healthy cities.

Hence: houses are not the panacea, and their logical consequence would be a dissolution of cities. *The aim is to deconcentrate, not to dissolve the city*. The extremes of city and country must be reconciled by making use of all our technical resources and by fully landscaping all available space on the ground and on roofs in order that nature may become a daily experience, not merely a Sunday excursion.

The construction of houses and high-rise apartment blocks must be developed simultaneously, each to the extent of its real demand. Wherever possible, the house should take the form of a one- or two-story structure in suburbs zoned for low density, while the high-rise apartment block should have an economical height of ten to twelve stories with centralized services, and it should be built wherever its effectiveness is proven, particularly in districts zoned for high density.

Walk-up apartments offer neither the advantages of the house nor those of the high-rise apartments, to which it is inferior socially, psychologically and in some respects even economically; their elimination will be welcome progress. In the last analysis, the future relative acceptance of the two remaining types of dwelling will depend on developing social and political trends.

12.

Organic Neighborhood Planning*

LACK of Integrated Pattern. With the development of the machine age the coherence and efficiency of the old community, which was characterized by the crafts, has rapidly disintegrated. The absence of a well-integrated, new community pattern that would fit the changed living conditions of the machine age is the most serious drawback to the promotion of genuine democratic growth.

The body called "society" is an indivisible entity which cannot function when some of its parts are not integrated or are being neglected; and when it does not function properly it will sicken.

Growing Social Indifference. The size of today's depersonalized mammoth city administrations has grown beyond human scale. A citizen of the city has no personal contact with his elected officials; he is obliged to surrender to a distant power. Consequently, growing social indifference has slackened community relations. Irresponsibility and social loneliness are

* See: "A Program for City Reconstruction" by W. Gropius & Martin Wagner, *The Architectural Forum,* New York, July 1943. *Rebuilding Our Communities* by W. Gropius, Paul Theobald, Chicago, 1945. *Organic Neighborhood Planning* by W. Gropius, *Housing and Town and Country Planning,* Bulletin No. 2, United Nations Department of Social Affairs, Lake Success, New York, April 1949.

spreading. Art, science and religion today are disconnected islands; a new synthesis must make whole again what is now, unhappily, separate.

Science, art and philosophy could supply the elements for a new order. Food, leisure and freedom could be had by all, but a workable method of collaboration and distribution has still to be found. Only when living in a well-integrated neighborhood can the citizen of today experience and learn the democratic procedure of give-and-take. Healthy neighborhood units are therefore the natural seed beds for improved human relations and higher standards of living. They help to develop a sense of community loyalty which finds expression in concerted action for social and civic progress.

Such a broad aim cannot be realized merely through "better housing." Housing, representing only one of many community functions, cannot be tackled unrelatedly without checking the capacity of the surrounding community to absorb new residential areas, and to provide good circulation and proper relationship between dwellings, working places and recreation areas. Otherwise our city features and techniques will begin to engulf our rural areas more and more, carrying with them the germs of our modern civic diseases: irresponsibility, deterioration of social contact, amorphous growth without coherence or distinctive form. Full consideration of an organic community plan as an indispensable framework has to precede any housing development. Without it, even new housing may turn rapidly into a blighted area and become a burdensome waste.

Sound community planning by local planning boards should be made the prerequisite of any public support for housing. Furthermore, the present trend toward decentralization has to be carefully watched lest it should lead back to scattered and unplanned housing.

Basic Community Pattern. Well-planned community rehabilitation seems to call first for drastic steps to stimulate community interest and responsibility on the part of every citizen by letting him participate actively in local affairs. To attain this goal, the administrative community framework must be humanized, that is, brought down to man size. It should be based on self-contained neighborhood units as distinct entities small enough to serve as organisms for reactivating social intercourse. After a generation of trial and error, architects and planners everywhere have agreed on this basic community pattern for the immediate future:

The smallest self-contained community unit—basic for urban and rural areas alike—should be the "neighborhood unit" with five to eight thousand inhabitants, which is a population large enough to assure efficient operation of an elementary school.

The next larger administrative unit should be a precinct or district in the city or a township in the country, each comprising a cluster of from five to ten neighborhood units—say, from 25,000 to 75,000 people—with a high school at its center.

Finally, the largest unit should be the entire city or metropolis with top-grade facilities for education and recreation.

Each self-contained neighborhood unit should have its own independent local government.

Such a scaled-down governmental setup would secure a more direct influence of the will of the people upon their administration and would also develop a sense of community spirit. Relations between families, friends and co-operative teams would have a better chance as creative factors in ordinary living. Direct participation in the corporate life of the unit would become a natural function of every citizen and would protect him against loneliness and isolation. Disregarding some few secluded hermits, man is a gregarious animal whose growth is always accelerated and improved by life in a healthy community. The reciprocal influence of individuals on each other is as essential to mental development as food is to the body. Left alone, without neighborly contact, the citizen's mind is dulled, its growth stunted.

The Human Point of View. In accordance with the humanly scaled local administration, the physical scale of such an organic social structure also must be human: that is, it must fit the cycle of the twenty-four-hour day, since men, not machines, determine the fundamental scale. Daily commuting time should total no more than thirty to forty minutes. The size of the neighborhood unit—whether rural or urban—should be confined to pedestrian distances, for the human stride ought to define the scope of local living space. All points of activity and interest in the neighborhood unit should be within ten to fifteen minutes' walking distance at the most. This would confine its size to an area with a radius of about one-half mile or less.

To be well balanced in itself, the basic unit requires working places for its inhabitants in separate business and industrial segments, as well as its own local administration, a shopping center and facilities for education, recreation and worship. Not one of these should be forgotten, for housing alone—a mere conglomeration of people—does not create an organic community. However, provided with communal facilities, every part of the unit being well related in size and location, the inhabitants would have a good chance to improve social contact, the prospect of which originally made urban life desirable. The social initiative of the people and their resourcefulness in organizing their own life would then originate at a local level and gradually reach out into a wider region.

New Regional Articulation. Through civic interest and loyalty growing from good relations within the immediate neighborhood and through healthy, competitive spirit and pride in achievement, regional articulation will again develop after having been lost in the industrial upheaval of the past. Delinquency and crime will also decrease with the improved social character of the neighborhood unit; for it has been found that social ills result from the lack of coherence and effectiveness of the social group rather than from biological or psychological factors, or even from poverty. Thus, a neighborhood unit, through forethought and the proper planning of well-integrated surroundings, has a good chance to build up its own identity and to retain and strengthen it. A good community plan cannot by itself create good neighborliness, but it can provide an environment full of potentialities.

Cultivation of the Social Soil. Such a statement has sound scientific background. Two English biologists, Dr. Scott Williamson and Dr. Ines Pearse, have done unique research in London's Peckham Health Center. They studied the structure of society in its smallest unit, which, according to them, is not the individual but the family. They found that nowhere could biologists study health as such, for everything was directed only toward the investigation of the sick. Consequently they created a platform upon which the possibilities of a rich, diversified social life could be offered to average families, affording the biologists an undistorted view of the factors supporting normal growth. In a specially designed, clublike building with swimming pool, cafeteria, nursery, gym and playrooms, hundreds of average London families found release from their previous social isolation. No experts were admitted and all the initiative for communal activities came from social intercourse among these families. No activities were forced on them, but plenty of opportunities were provided by the right type of building. The only requirement for membership was a periodic health overhaul.

The record of their experiment shows that "health grows and spreads not by treatment of sickness, not by prevention of disease, nor primarily by any form of correction of physical or social ills, but through cultivation of the social soil."

According to them health, if given a chance to spread, is just as "infectious" as disease. And they find that a community is not formed merely by an accumulation of persons for the convenience of sustaining some ulterior purpose, as in a housing project connected with a large industrial plant. Rather it is the result of a natural, functional organization in society. As it grows, it determines its own anatomy and physiology according to biological law. Thus a community is a specific "organ" of the body of society, formed of living and growing cells—the homes which compose it.

The heart of the communal organism, co-ordinating the potentialities for a rich, diversified life, is the neighborhood civic center from which branch out the social arteries that determine the character and strength of the whole group. Initially such a center requires a meeting hall and some committee rooms and could best be developed in connection with the school. Here the people themselves can direct their daily life in contact with all age groups and have influence in the administration as well as in the cultural activities. As a social nucleus, the civic center gives direction and stimulation to concentrated group efforts, and at the same time enables each individual, through active participation, to attain his full stature within the community.

Priority for Community Center. *Since these small community centers are instruments of such vital importance to the human development of the group, they should be given priority over any other rehabilitation scheme, even over housing.* Like the powerhouse of an industrial plant, they generate the current for the vital arteries of the group.

Everywhere community improvement can be speeded up by adopting an organic sequence in the planning procedure, that is, by creating two essential preconditions: the setting up of new neighborhood units, urban or rural, and their boundaries, each unit to have its independent local government; and the erection, in a central position, of a small community center within each of these units, preferably in connection with the school building. This would establish a sound, humanly scaled framework with an immediate political significance.

Procedure and Sequence in Community Planning. What sequence of procedure should we employ to break the vicious circle choking our cities? As they need relief from congestion, from "high blood pressure," we should first siphon out those people who cannot be permanently employed in the city and offer to resettle them, together with some smaller industries, in neighborhood units to be built in the country. I want to emphasize that such a policy requires the transfer of endangered production as well as purchasing power from sore spots in the city to a sound new area. There stranded workers can be reclaimed for production at a much lower cost per capita than the old city would need to pay for slum clearance on expensive land and for unproductive relief. Such a transfer of idle labor would relieve the sick body of the old city, improve its circulation and open up the recreation space for its rejuvenation.

The open spaces thus regained in the city could be used for the erection of necessary communal facilities and park areas, and for a basic net of traffic arteries connecting the neighborhood districts with each other and with the civic centers. Freed of dead weight, the reopened areas of the dying cities could then be returned to their proper functions as integral parts of an organic social structure for the whole region. Such a development would, of course, take time.

From the planning of neighborhood units in the open country—the initial step in the process of reconstruction—we should be able to gather enough experience to manage the much more difficult second step of developing new community structures within the old cities.

Suggestions for a Practicable Reconstruction Procedure: *

1. Lot and block rehabilitation has not been successful. Sweeping "square mile" rehabilitation has become a necessity since we have recognized the interrelationship of the town with its region.

2. Former suggestions such as "The City Beautiful" and other pictorial schemes have proved to be incomplete. First, action should be started by preparing legal, financial and administrative instruments to enable the planners to conceive and work out reliable master plans.

3. Places of work and their relation to places of living should form the pivot of all reconstruction work.

* From: "A Program for City Reconstruction" by Walter Gropius & Martin Wagner, *The Architectural Forum,* July 1943.

4. First of all the existing cities should be relieved of congestion and high blood pressure by removing those who cannot be permanently employed. Resettled around small industries in new "townships" these people would regain their productive capacity and purchasing power.

5. The new townships should settle along superhighways and be connected by fast feeder roads with the old city center.

6. The size of the townships should be limited by the pedestrian range to keep them within a human scale.

7. The townships must be surrounded by their own farm belts.

8. Speculation often promotes blight and obsolescence. Therefore the community should own the land. The dwelling lots should be rented, though the house may be owned.

9. The administrative setup of a township should take the form of a self-contained unit with its independent local government. This will strengthen community spirit.

10. From five to ten—or more—neighborhood townships may be combined into a countyship with an administration governing activities beyond the reach of a single unit. Its size and administrative setup should also serve as a model for the basic neighborhood units of the old towns to be reconstructed.

11. It is suggested that the size of a township remain stable. Flexibility within its boundaries must therefore be achieved by making the housing facilities elastic.

12. Parallel to the resettlement of idle labor in new townships, a second process must take place; acquisition of land by the community of the old city. For not until that process of pooling land has been completed can the next step—the redistribution of land—be taken for the final reconstruction of the city.

A fundamental framework as outlined above would constitute a sound basis for building up a town pattern fit for the twentieth-century machine age from the social as well as from the economic and cultural points of view.

13.

Problems of the "Core"
(Community Center)*

I AM deeply convinced that *the building of community centers is of even greater urgency than housing itself, for these centers represent a cultural breeding ground which enables the individual to attain his full stature within the community.*

Different countries have found different answers to what actually constitutes a community center, a "core," according to their varying hereditary habits and traditions, their stage of technical development and the natural setting in which they find themselves. The Latin countries, for instance, have, early in their history, developed clearly defined plazas in which the life of the community centered and found its expression, while the Anglo-Saxon civilization has made comparatively little use of such public centers, favoring, instead, the individual home as meeting ground for most social intercourse.

This is, of course, partly due to the difference in climatic conditions, but not entirely so. Regional preferences and imponderables must be given careful consideration when attempting new solutions and, in many cases, it will be necessary first to reawaken a demand for community centers because

---

* See: CIAM, *The Heart of the City,* Pellegrini & Cudahy, New York, 1952.

they have disappeared from the scene to such a degree that people do not even remember their great advantages for the individual and the communal life.

In former, more settled periods of history such public centers grew either naturally by public demand or by decree of a potentate, but they were never neglected as they are so often in the present, particularly in those countries that stand in the forefront of industrial and technical development. While we equip the individual home with every conceivable amenity we have overlooked the merits of the public meeting place; we have surrendered our streets and public spaces almost entirely to the automobile, and the pedestrian, forced to withdraw to a narrow sidewalk, has lost his right of way. The important neighborly contact which had been so basic for the coherence of the old cities and towns has been destroyed by the explosive force of vehicular traffic. It is important that we should re-establish in our communities public centers where people, undisturbed by traffic, can rub elbows in a neutral atmosphere that is not dominated by the influence of the private home and where the spirit of the community can find its public expression.

The most famous example of a beautiful core which for centuries has served its community most effectively as receptacle for its public life is the Piazza St. Marco in Venice. It expressed the greatness of God in its cathedral, the power of the doge in its palace; the tower was a symbol the sailors could see from the sea; but most of all it was the big drawing room of the people, the public stage of the town for festivities, parades and religious ceremonies. When we look at the modern plaza in front of the UN buildings in New York we find that it is hardly used as a community center; it is more a monumental approach to the entrances. Rockefeller Center in New York offers a small community core which promotes some exchange between people, but its value is impaired by the roar of traffic passing by. In a modern city plazas for pedestrians seem to be more necessary than ever before, for here, in daily contact and exchange among people grow the grass roots of democracy.

Why does one core within a town or city attract us as pleasant when another may not? The intricate problem of scale lies at the bottom of this question. A good solution much depends on whether a harmonious relationship has been achieved between the height of the surrounding buildings and the dimensions of the plaza. The actual size of the plaza should barely accommodate the peak hour of activity. If it is too large it will look empty and may never provide the contagious atmosphere and liveliness so essential for its success. Gigantic, undivided open spaces leave most people intimidated rather than stimulated.

I have found that if a harmony has been created between open spaces and surrounding building masses such a well-balanced composition can even absorb discordant details. In the cores of old towns we find also that very different individual buildings, often centuries apart and of different styles, are living side by side in complete harmony as parts of an organic whole. This harmony, however, is not the result of a "matching" process; the design of a new building which was to be added to the existing old ones was invariably conceived as part of the greater whole into which it had to fit harmoniously, but contemporary means of expression were used, not borrowed style motives of past periods.

One problem that inevitably arises in connection with the

planning of community centers is whether its buildings should have a "monumental" expression. The controversy over the definition of monumentality and whether monuments are an "eternal" need of mankind is obviously caused by the acute drama of transformation of all our inherited values that our generation is faced with. Disregarding the pseudo-monumentalism of imitative eclecticism which is slowly coming to a halt like a flywheel whose motoric force has long since died, the accepted meaning of the word "monument" is a memorial of huge size, symbolizing something worth commemorating—religious faith, an important event, a great man, a social accomplishment. *Rather than on its size I should like to put the emphasis on the spiritual meaning of a monument, on its artistic conception and grandeur, on those intangibles which are likely to stir the imagination.* The very idea of resuming monumental expression through static form symbols as in the past should be alien to the creative mind of our period. The monument of former times was the symbol for a static conception of the world, replaced today by a new one of relative values. I believe, therefore, that the equivalent for monumental expression will develop in the direction of a new physical pattern for a higher form of civic life, a pattern characterized by its adaptability for continuous growth and change. To give a more concrete example for such a statement: The Tennessee Valley Development in the United States, representing a new, collective effort to organically improve the whole setup of a community and its administration, will, I believe, contribute more toward a monumental expression of our time and will inspire more civic self-respect and loyalty than the imposing size of an Empire State Building, a mere quantitative symbol of expediency.

But higher spiritual aspirations of a growing culture, reaching beyond utilitarian aspects and worth to be visibly interpreted by the architect and the artist, develop only slowly, subconsciously. When the prevailing philosophy of "time is money" will yield to a humanly higher civilization—then the reconquest of the "monumental" will be at hand. But it will not come back as the "frozen music" of static symbols; it will become, instead, an inherent quality of our whole man-made environment.

14.

Housing Industry*

MAN is undoubtedly endowed with the capability of building his dwelling soundly and adequately, but innate inertia and sentimental attachment to tradition are obstructing his progress. The austerity occasioned by world events is today forcing governments as well as individuals to surmount this inertia. By adjusting to changed world conditions, attempts are finally being made to realize the old ideal of building typical dwellings more cheaply, better and in larger numbers than heretofore so as to provide every family with the basis for a healthy life. Generally applicable solutions genuinely suited to modern conditions have not yet been found, simply because the problem of dwelling design as such has never been dealt with in its entirety of sociological, economic, technical and formal ramifications. Starting from scratch, it must be solved on a large-scale basis by a systematic consideration of these factors. All previous attempts were deadlocked on controversial side issues, on matters of "ersatz" materials and economy construction measures, on agricultural or esthetic

* See: *Bauhausbücher,* Vol. 3, *Ein Versuchshaus des Bauhauses,* Albert Langen Verlag, München, 1924.

Though this article was written thirty years ago I have included it in this book, because I still consider it essentially valid after extended practical experiences in prefabrication.

deliberations. However, as soon as the over-all scope of preconceived requirements which affect the dwelling design problem are clearly recognized and accurately outlined, the tactical problem of realization is reduced to a mere problem of methods and large-scale management.

This universal ideal of "how do we want to live?" as a generally applicable result of reflections upon the spiritual and material possibilities of our age has not yet been clearly outlined. The chaotic lack of unity of our residential buildings is evidence of the vagueness of prevailing concepts concerning the proper dwelling for modern man.

Is it a reflection of man's way of life that each individual's dwelling should differ entirely from that of every other individual? Is it not a sign of intellectual impoverishment and fallacious thinking to furnish a dwelling in rococo or Renaissance style while identical modern clothes are worn in all parts of the world? Advances in technology made during the past three generations surpass those of millennia before us. The better we organize physical labor, the more the human spirit will be emancipated. Perhaps mobile dwellings which will enable us to take with us all the conveniences of comfortable living even when we move are no longer utopian.

Housing the people is a problem of mass requirements. Who would dream of having his shoes custom made? Instead, we buy stock products which satisfy most individual requirements, thanks to refined production methods. Similarly, it will be possible for the individual in the future to order from stock dwellings suitable for his purposes. Modern technique might already be ripe for this development, but the building trade today is still using old methods of handcrafts in which the machine plays only a subordinate role. A radical reformation of the entire building trade along industrial lines is therefore a must for a modern solution of this important problem. It must be simultaneously approached from the three angles of economy, technology and form; all three are interdependent. Satisfactory results can only be gained by simultaneous progress in all three fields because of the profusion of complex problems involved. These are beyond the competence of the individual and can be solved only by a concerted effort in collaboration with numerous experts.

Reduction of cost of dwelling construction is of decisive importance for the national budget. Attempts to reduce the cost of conventional handicraft methods of construction by introducing more rigorous organizational techniques have brought only slight progress. The problem was not attacked at its root. The new aim, on the other hand, would be the manufacture by mass production methods of stock dwellings which are no longer constructed at the site but are produced in special factories in the form of component parts or units suitable for assembly. The advantages of this method of production would be increasingly greater in the extent to which it becomes possible to assemble such prefabricated component parts of houses at the building site just like machines. This dry assembly method, to be discussed in detail below, would eliminate not only the troublesome twisting and warping of building parts due to moisture but also the loss of time required for the drying out of houses built by conventional construction methods of masonry, mortar and plaster. This would at once ensure independence of weather and season.

An industrial building process of this type is only conceivable on a broad financial basis. The small individual contractor, engineer or architect will never be in the position to realize such building techniques alone by himself. On the other hand, large enterprises involving all the separate branches under a single ownership have been found to be economically feasible in other fields of business as well. It would therefore be necessary first to mobilize a large number of interested people before consumer organizations and vertical enterprises could be formed whose financial strength would be adequate to ensure the realization of such a major project. Of course, the economic advantages of this industrialized construction method would then be enormous. Experienced experts estimate that savings of 50 per cent or more can be expected. This would imply that every employed person could then afford to provide his family with a good, healthful dwelling, just as he can nowadays purchase the articles of daily need at less cost due to the development of world industry than this was possible for previous generations. The cost of these industrial products could be reduced step by step by the use of steam and electric power increasingly replacing hand labor; cost reduction in the construction industry will equally depend upon the exploitation of such power.

The other important means of cost reduction is based on new farsighted financing policies which should consciously avoid excessive interest rates on the building capital due to unproductive middlemen dispensable in the transaction.

Before decisive preliminary organizational steps can be taken toward solving the industrial mass production problem, our living requirements must be clarified sufficiently to establish generally valid, precise demands as to "how do we want to live?" As a result, numerous habits will be found to be superfluous and obsolete; for example, it should be no loss to reduce the size of rooms in favor of increasing living comforts. *The majority of citizens of a specific country have similar dwelling and living requirements; it is therefore hard to understand why the dwellings we build should not show a similar unification as, say, our clothes, shoes or automobiles.* The danger of undesirable suppression of legitimate individual requirements should be no greater here than in the case of fashions.

There is no justification for the fact that every house in a suburban development should have a different floor plan, a different exterior of a different style and different building materials; on the contrary, this is a wasteful and tasteless attitude of parvenus. The old farmhouse as well as the average citizen's town house of the eighteenth century, for example, all throughout Europe, show a similar arrangement of the floor plan and the over-all design. However, the danger of too rigid a standardization, such as is exemplified by the English suburban home, must be avoided because suppression of individuality is always shortsighted and unwise. Dwellings must be designed in such a way that justified individual requirements derived from the family size or the type of profession of the family head can be suitably and flexibly fulfilled. *The organization must therefore aim first of all at standardizing and mass-producing not entire houses, but only their component parts which can then be assembled into various types of houses, in the same way as in modern machine design certain internationally standardized parts are interchangeably used for different machines.* The production policy would provide for carrying in stock all individual parts necessary for the construction of houses of various types and sizes, to be ordered to the building site as required from various specialized factories. At the same time field-tested assembly plans for houses of different layout and appearance will be available to the public. Since all the standardized machine-made parts will fit together accurately, house erection at the site on the basis of precise assembly plans can be performed rapidly and with a minimum of labor, partly with unskilled workers, and under any conditions of weather and season. Above all, this method avoids once and for all the numerous embarrassing surprises and unpredictable hazards which are inevitably connected with the conventional methods of construction: failure of building elements to fit due to inaccurate wall dimensions or to the effects of moisture, unforeseen patchwork due to construction damage, loss of time and rent due to delays in drying, as well as the consequences of the usual haste in the design of custom-made house plans. Instead, we shall be blessed with exact fit of the various machine-made component building parts, with a fixed price, and with a brief, accurately predictable and guaranteed assembly time for the house.

The realization of this economic and organizational scheme is above all the engineer's problem. Also from his point of view the task represents a radical change from conventional developments in regard to building materials as well as structural design. Most construction today is executed with the old natural building materials, stone, brick and wood. Production of most of the old house takes place at the building site. The necessary tools and machinery, while being transported to the site for this purpose, block the traffic. These mobile factories, so to speak, are necessarily primitive compared to stationary plants. Erection of the building shell by conventional methods makes it impossible to predict the time required for the rough enclosure to dry and the interior to be completed because this depends upon weather conditions. Attempts to perfect these conventional building methods, for example by enlarging the building blocks and introducing more highly standardized and efficient organization of the work at the site, failed to achieve significant simplifications or cost reductions. In order to reap the advantages of the new assembly construction methods, industry will therefore have to employ building materials other than those used heretofore, materials capable of being processed by machine instead of unprocessed natural materials. In this respect the aim would not be the creation of substitutes, but the improvement of natural products to obtain absolutely reliable uniformity of performance (rolled steel, cement alloys, synthetic wood). A standardized solution of the problem would be made possible only by prefabrication of all the structural parts necessary in the construction of a house, even the walls, ceilings and roof.

To this end, the structural design of houses must also be changed drastically. Either a material must be produced which possesses the same structural and insulating properties as conventional masonry walls while having less volume and weight so that it can be assembled in large slabs of story height, or else the whole structure must be made of a structural skeleton on the one hand and of nonstructural wall, roof and ceiling panels on the other. A skeleton of this type may be of steel beams and columns or of reinforced concrete beams and pillars connected to different structural systems similar to wood frame constructions. The panels for the walls, ceilings and roof will have to consist of standardized slabs which are to be factory-made of weather-resistant material, dimensionally stable, yet porous, insulating, tough and of light weight. Building slabs of this nature are already beginning to appear on the market in the form of the conventional planks of pumice concrete or gypsum. But the problems involved in the industrial production of satisfactory wall, ceiling and roof panels, as well as of a suitable light skeleton for houses, are still in need of an economical solution. The standardization and mass production of doors, windows, stairs, trim, fixtures and interior finish has already reached a more advanced stage of development, although hand labor still outweighs industrial machine production. The engineer engaged in vehicular design for railroad cars, ships, automobiles and airplanes has surpassed the building engineer in the development of his methods of construction and materials insofar as he has already perfected the use of machine-processed, homogeneous building materials (iron, aluminum, glass) and the application of machine-produced structural components made of such materials. His experience is therefore of inestimable value in the field of housing mass production.

The new building method should meet with approval from the artistic standpoint as well. *It is fallacious to assume that architecture will deteriorate because of the industrialization of dwelling construction. On the contrary, the standardization of building elements will have the beneficial effect of imparting a unified character to new dwellings and developments.* There is no reason to fear monotony such as that of English suburbs, provided the basic requirement is fulfilled of standardizing only the building elements, whereas the appearance of buildings assembled from these elements will vary. The form of these elements shall be determined solely by their purpose and function. Their "beauty" should be ensured by good, well-finished materials and lucid, simple design, not by added-on decorations and profiles alien to their structural or material properties. The success with which these building elements, this large-scale "erector set," are assembled into an actual structure of well-proportioned space depends upon the creative talents of the designing architect. The standardization of parts certainly does not limit the variety of individual arrangements which we all desire, and the recurrence of individual parts and identical materials in the various buildings will have a rhythmic and soothing effect on us. Adequate freedom remains for individual or national character to express itself, exactly as in the case of our clothing, and yet all of it will bear the stamp of our era.

As extensive a project as the industrialization of building construction can only be carried out with the aid of an unusual extent of public support. The problem is of such great importance to national economy that laymen and experts alike must emphatically demand that the government make preparations for its solution on a public level. States and communities, being the major builders, are compelled economically and culturally to exploit all possible means for reducing the cost of housing construction. The previous approach of encouraging the use of "ersatz" materials and short-cut methods of construction has failed to reach the goal. Publicly supported experimental building sites are needed! Any article to be mass-produced by industry must be systematically subjected to numerous preliminary tests in which the businessman, the engineer and the artist participate equally before its model is standardized for production; similarly the production of standardized building components can be accomplished only by large-scale collaboration among industrialists, economists and artists. Teamwork so organized, not the creation of "ersatz" methods, would represent genuine planning and economic foresight.

It is obvious that construction of the pilot model houses will require considerable investment, just as do the models made in industrial laboratories as a basis for mass-produced consumer goods. The financing of these experiments is the task of the consumer organizations which are to benefit from the savings to be achieved ultimately. They are the organizations primarily interested in the establishment of experimental institutions where all previous accomplishments can be systematically collected in accordance with guiding principles and be tested with a view to the new building rationale. So drastic a modification of the building industry is bound to take place gradually, to be sure. But in spite of all arguments against such development, it will inevitably come. The enormous waste of materials, time and labor, caused by the fact that extensive housing developments are still being built by hand according to countless unrelated individual designs instead of being mass-produced according to standardized though flexible plans, can no longer be defended on any grounds.

15.

A Way Out of the Housing Confusion*

THE idea of eliminating waste by rationalization has permeated the modern life of communities and individuals alike. But rationalization must not be mixed up with ability to produce profit, for social requirements of the population, as well as economic problems, are involved.

The rationalization of building should imply collecting, concentrating and unifying all isolated efforts for the various building activities in order to obtain a general plan covering the building field.

Creative research for improvement and refinement can become effective only by systematic organization of the existing material and mental equipment applied to the process of building and by their mutual interrelation. Most delay in the progress of modern building is caused by lack of unification.

Housing, the most urgent and also the most complicated building problem, illustrates this statement strikingly: Today, the main task of the building profession—socially and technically—is to build up an adequate service to provide

---

* See: "Toward a Living Architecture" by W. Gropius, *American Architect & Architecture,* New York, February 1938. *Memorandum for the House Committee Investigating National Defense Migration* by W. Gropius & Martin Wagner, U.S. 77th Congress, 1st session, 1941, Vol. 17, pp. 6949–56.

sufficient, decent, up-to-date dwellings for the community. These buildings, which have to satisfy the material and psychical requirements of life, must be constructed at the lowest possible expense of time and material, and at a price the average man can afford. Is this sort of dwelling on the market? No, it is not. Although the average man buys his food, his clothing and his other everyday goods at a reasonable price, adapted to his income, the only dwelling he can obtain is an obsolete building originally built for more wealthy people, and now out of date. Even the rent of government-supported housing developments with public subsidy is still too high to be afforded by the lower-income class.

Something must be wrong with the whole building trade if the rent of even these dwellings, only about half paid for by their tenants, remains out of reach of the poorest. Here it becomes evident why the market is not interested in building dwellings for the average man in spite of the wide demand. Prices and rents, which give the builders and owners of dwellings a good profit, are far out of proportion to the prices of all the other articles in daily use which are well adapted to the average income. What is the reason for this devitalizing process? What must be changed in the economic structure in order to rebalance the market price of adequate dwellings?

In 1928, I found in the U.S.A. a most illuminating diagram, roughly comparing the trend of prices for building and for automobiles between 1913 and 1926. It shows the remarkable fact that within the same period the average costs of building were doubled, whereas the price of the Ford car was halved. The greater proportion of handwork involved in building increased the price in accordance with the increasing labor costs. Refinement of mass production methods, on the other hand, considerably lowered the price of automobiles. A decent dwelling became unattainable for the low-income class, yet the car became an everyman's tool. The up-to-date completion of the diagram shows that the price of the average car has steadily declined, whereas the cost of the average dwelling has been only slightly lowered since 1926. This diagram reveals that our building methods, being far behind the times, are not yet fit to solve the problem.

As building is the most extensive and complicated field of human production, it could not keep pace with the development of the machine—and it is the last field to be conquered by it. Further, there is no balanced organization of the building trades yet, as there is in other industries; it is still rather tied up with handwork and individual management which, forced into competition with industrial methods, have lost their former quality and efficiency. Although more and more parts of the building are constantly being made by machine, progress is hampered by lack of comprehensiveness, with which this problem should be attacked as a whole. For this is not a problem of mere manufacturing. Surely mass production methods must eventually permeate the building trade; but deep changes in the economic structure are indispensable before the market will be ready for prefabrication on a large scale. The first enthusiasm toward prefabrication has calmed down, after many drawbacks have given evidence that no single person or single firm alone can solve that gigantic task as Ford solved it for the automobile. The solution of this problem seems to be self-evident; yet, it is so deeply rooted in our economic structure that the community as a whole can master it only by attacking it from all angles simultaneously. It is, first of all, a problem of integration. Much time will be gained, therefore, if a comprehensive scheme of action is set up by the best experts, co-operating in all the many fields of building activity. A guiding key plan offers authoritative significance which should direct the future efforts toward housing. The many brilliant private efforts, now lost by isolation and lack of power, must be united.

It is obvious that private enterprise, in its struggle for existence, is bound to overemphasize subjective interests. A public institute, however, would be apt to investigate more objectively all sorts of ideas and inventions and their practicability for the good of the commonwealth. Only technological approach, undisturbed by any political or private interference, can set a high standard.

An "Institute of Building Integration" should be created, in which federal, state and municipal authorities would co-operate with architects, engineers, contractors, manufacturers, realtors, bankers and trade-unionists as their advisers, to produce a final solution of the pressing need for adequate housing. All the existing institutions for public and private research in building practice should co-operate, exchanging their experiences and results, simultaneously acquiring a better knowledge of the difficulties of correlated problems. The key plan to be set up by such an institute would aim at embracing everything expected to raise the social standard, to decrease the prices of houses, and to secure their movability in accordance with the fluctuation of the working places. Primary considerations would involve:

Regulating regional planning by interstate legislation, e.g., zoning ordinances.

Furthering the lease of land for housing for limited periods.

Preparing the investment market for prefabrication and for the new idea of a housing service (shorter amortization and lower interests).

Improving building regulations by adapting them to new building techniques.

Research for socially and economically most suitable types of dwelling.

Research for suitable standard sizes of the component parts of dwellings; these parts to be interchangeable for different types of houses.

Research for actual prefabrication, including mechanical units such as kitchen, bathroom, heating and air-conditioning plant.

Simplification of the building organization in offices and at the site.

There are many brilliant attempts made in these various fields, but they are rather isolated from one another instead of being parts of a well-tuned organism which is so badly needed. The suggested Institute of Building Integration should fill this gap but, as so much organization work would be involved, the idea of rationalization must be safeguarded against red tape which would stunt its only aim—namely, to promote creative progress.

The cost of such an institute, to be put up by the government, would be irrelevant when compared with the savings to be expected from economizing on housing costs throughout the country by such means of concentration and integration. The efficiency of money spent for housing could probably be doubled and bring the key problem of social welfare close to its final solution, simultaneously increasing private initiative and employment.

IV.

Scope of Total Architecture

16.

Scope of Total Architecture*

CENTURY of Science. I have tried to summarize for myself what the changes are that have taken place during my
own lifetime in the physical as well as in the spiritual world.
When I was a boy, my family lived in a city apartment with
open gas jets, individual coal-heated stoves in each room,
including the bathroom, where warm water was heated for
the bath each Saturday: that took two hours. There was no
electric streetcar, no automobile, no plane. Radio, film,
gramophone, X-ray, telephone were nonexistent.

The mental climate which prevailed in the eighties and
nineties was still more or less of a static character. It rotated
around a seemingly unshakable conception of eternal truths.
How rapidly has this conception been fading away, changing
into that of a world of incessant transmutation, of mutually
dependent phenomena. Time and space have become coef-
ficients of one and the same cosmic force.

The sum of all these tremendous changes that took place
during the last half-century of industrial development has
achieved a more sweeping transformation of human life than

* See: *Architecture and Design in the Age of Science* by W. Gropius,
The Spiral Press, New York, 1952. *Rebuilding Our Communities* by W.
Gropius, Paul Theobald, Chicago, 1945. *Faith in Planning* by W. Gropius,
Planning, 1952, American Society of Planning Officials. Chicago.

those of all the centuries since Jesus Christ combined. Small wonder, then, that we feel the strain of this superhuman speed of development which seems to be out of step with the natural inertia of the human heart and with our limited power of adaptation.

Every thinking contemporary searches his mind now trying to figure out what may be the ultimate value of our stupendous scientific progress. We roar with new techniques and new inventions for speedier means of transportation. But what do we do with all the time saved? Do we use it for contemplation of our existence? No, we plunge instead into an even more hectic current of activity, surrendering to that fallacious slogan: time is money. We obviously need a clarification as to what exactly our spiritual and intellectual aims are.

Some time ago I read an article by Leo Tolstoy in which he reproaches science for studying purposely "everything." He held that mankind cannot possibly pay attention to "everything" and that we are going to tear ourselves to pieces, trying to go in a hundred different directions at the same time, unless we find out what we want most and make that the goal of our supreme effort. Of course, he thought of religion giving that final direction which establishes beyond a shadow of a doubt what should come first, after which everything else falls into place almost automatically. Well, if it isn't religion, what is it? Science has come a long way since Tolstoy's time and there are people who seriously believe that it can be the final arbiter and pass judgment on good and evil. Even if we should come to believe this, we would still have to make up our mind as to which scientific concept we want to give free rein, because, applied simultaneously, they may easily force each other out of existence and we would be the losers.

Strategic Aim.   I should like, therefore, to attempt to outline the potential strategic aim of planning for my own profession, architecture, within the cultural and political context of our industrial civilization. I shall try first to give a definition: *Good planning I conceive to be both a science and an art. As a science, it analyzes human relationships; as an art, it co-ordinates human activities into a cultural synthesis.* I want to put the emphasis particularly on the art of planning. Here, I believe, lie waiting creative potentialities that would give meaning and direction to our countless, isolated efforts.

We talk so much about the fact that the rapid development of science has cut so sharply into the familiar pattern of our existence that we are left with nothing but loose ends. In his eternal curiosity man learned to dissect his world with the scalpel of the scientist, and in the process has lost his balance and his sense of unity. Our scientific age, by going to extremes of specialization, has obviously prevented us from seeing our complicated life as an entity. The average professional man, driven to distraction by the multiplicity of problems spread out before him, seeks relief from the pressure of general responsibilities by picking out one single, rigidly circumscribed responsibility in a specialized field and refuses to be answerable for anything that may happen outside this field. A general dissolution of context has set in and naturally resulted in shrinking and fragmentating life. As Albert Einstein once put it: "Perfection of means and confusion of aims seem to be characteristic of our age."

Task of Reunification.   But there are indications that we are slowly moving away from overspecialization and its perilous atomizing effect on the social coherence of the community. If we skim the mental horizon of our present civilization, we observe that many ideas and discoveries are wholly concerned with finding again the relationship between the phenomena of the universe, which scientists had so far viewed only in isolation from neighboring fields. Medicine is building up the psychosomatic approach to treatment of diseases, acknowledging the mutual interdependence of psyche and soma, the body. The physicist has contributed new knowledge of the identity of matter and energy. The artist has learned to express visibly with inert materials a new dimension—time and motion. Are we on the way to regain a comprehensive vision of the oneness of the world which we had taken apart? In the gigantic task of its reunification, the planner and architect will have to play a big role. He must be well trained not ever to lose a total vision, in spite of the infinite wealth of specialized knowledge which he has to absorb and integrate. He must comprehend land, nature, man and his art, as one great entity. In our mechanized society we should passionately emphasize that we are still a world of men, that man in his natural environment must be the focus of all planning. We have indulged our latest pets, the machines, to such an extent that we have lost a genuine scale of values. Therefore, we need to investigate what makes up the really worth-while relationships among men, and between men and nature, instead of giving way to the pressure of special interests or of shortsighted enthusiasts who want to make mechanization an end in itself.

Whom are we going to house? The people, of course, and that includes everybody. It injures the functions of our whole society if we neglect any part of it. The sickness of our present

grow into a commonly recognized form of expression, both physically and spiritually. The great avalanche of science and progress has left the individual bewildered and restless, unable to adjust himself and often pitifully lacking in moral initiative. We have developed a Gallup Poll mentality, a mechanistic conception; we rely on quantity instead of on quality, on memory instead of on ideas; we yield to expediency instead of forming a new conviction.

Artist: Prototype of "Whole Man."   Is there an antidote to this trend? Our society has certainly recognized the essential value of the scientist for its survival. We are very little aware, however, of the vital importance of the creative artist when it comes to controlling and shaping our environment. In contrast to the process of mechanization, the work of the true artist consists of an unprejudiced search for expression that symbolizes the common phenomena of life. This requires that he take an independent, uninhibited view of the whole life process. His work is most essential for the development of a true democracy, for he is the prototype of "whole" man; his freedom and independence are relatively intact. His intuitive qualities should be the antidote against overmechanization, apt to rebalance our life and to humanize the impact of the machine. Unfortunately the artist has become the forgotten man, almost ridiculed and thought of as a superfluous luxury member of society. *My belief is that, on the contrary, our disoriented society badly needs participation in the arts as an essential counterpart of science in order to stop its atomistic effect on us.*

Examining our own experiences, we know that it is only in isolated cases that sober scientific facts can, all by themselves, stir the imagination to a point where people become willing to subordinate cherished personal ambitions to a common cause. Much deeper chords must be struck than those reached by analytical information if we want to call forth an enthusiastic, contagious response, capable of sweeping away barriers that stand now in the way of better planning and housing. Though scientific progress has reached us in the form of materialistic abundance and physical well-being, it has rarely matured into producing form. Consequently we find that our emotional demands remain unsatisfied by the mere material production of the eight-hour working day. This failure to gladden the soul must be the reason why we have not always been able to make our brilliant scientific and technical achievements count, and why a cultural pattern that should have emerged has, so far, eluded us.

I am convinced, therefore, that the contribution of the creative designer whose art can realize more fully the visual aspects and the human appeal of planning is essential. No society of the past has produced cultural expression without the participation of the artist; social problems cannot be solved through intellectual processes or political action only. I speak of the great necessity to recover through every man's education the lost quality of understanding and creating form.

Think of those essential imponderables, apparent in cities and towns of bygone cultures, which still have the power to move us emotionally today, though they are obsolete from the point of view of practical use. These imponderables characterize what is missing in the concept of our present communities, namely, that unity of order and spirit which is forever significant, visibly expressed in space and volume.

Lack of Responsive Audience.   Can a child, growing up in "Main Street," be expected to be in the habit of looking for beauty? He hasn't met with it yet and wouldn't even know what to ask for because his perceptive faculties have been blunted from the beginning by the ruthless assault of the chaotic colors, shapes and noises of modern salesmanship. He is left in a constant state of sensorial apathy, finally hardening into that intractable citizen who has ceased to be even aware of his impoverished surroundings. As often as not it is from this background, though, that the potential architectural client emerges, and it becomes immediately evident why he so rarely rises above creating anything but a blur or a sham when trying to give form to his environment.

None of our magnificent, practical new tools can turn "Main Street" into a beautiful pattern for living unless they are put into creative hands, unless a changing attitude of mind will bring about a fusion between science and art. But at which end shall we start to bring this about? Because what we need is not only the creative artist, but a responsive audience and how are we going to get it? Only by a slow educational process, providing comprehensive experience from early childhood on. It means, in short, that we must start at the kindergarten to make children playfully reshape their immediate environment. For participation is the key word in planning. Participation sharpens individual responsibility, the prime factor in making a community coherent, in developing group vision and pride in the self-created environment. *Such educational conception would put book knowledge in its right place, as an auxiliary only to experience in action, which alone can lead to constructive attitudes and habits of thought.* Any information given to a citizen after he has been exposed as a youth to educational practices that made planning seem everybody's concern will fall on fertile ground.

Planners experience in their daily work that the public is still very ignorant of the great benefits awaiting it from good planning. The average citizen is inclined to see an interference with his personal freedom when given direction by government agencies. The necessity continuously to inform him why communal planning is to his own best advantage calls for the highest psychological ability in a planner. A systematic psychological training in "basic politics" should give the planning student the understanding of cause and effect of human behavior. It should teach him how to put into his own practice persuasion, tact, patience and appreciation of the thought and position of others as the most effective tools of planning. It should tend to give him greater flexibility of mind, the resiliency of an alert wrestler, always ready to adjust to unpredictable situations. It should fulfill the need to develop a definite attitude of the student beyond his acquisition of the necessary knowledge and techniques.

Today we still meet too often with a deep-rooted inclination to dodge a large-scale conception for planning and housing and to add up, instead, unrelated piecemeal improvements. This will change only with a growing community spirit, carefully nurtured on all educational levels until it becomes a subconscious attitude of everybody and may finally cause a chain reaction conducive to solving our collective task.

Needed: Experiments in Living. Such an educational framework, as here indicated, also seems to have qualities favorable for the advancement of genuine teamwork which will naturally develop more and more in the future with the ever widening horizon of our physical knowledge of which each of us commands only a small segment. The task is too big for individuals alone. After almost twenty-five years of most valuable research and formulation of our ideas, we seem now to be in urgent need of action in groups. For in spite of the wealth of theoretical thought on community living which has been accumulated in recent years, hardly any new comprehensive "experiments in living" have been made. There is no other way toward progress but to start courageously and without prejudice new practical tests by building model communities in one stroke and then systematically examining their living value. What a wealth of new information for the sociologist, the economist, the scientist and the artist would be forthcoming, if groups, formed of the most able planners and architects available, should be commissioned to design and build completely new model communities! Such information would also offer most valuable preparatory data to solve the complicated problem of rehabilitating our existing communities. The blocks which have to be removed before we can create such laboratories for living are obviously political and legal in character. Without duly accepted legal instruments, one community master plan after the other will become a symbol of wishful thinking, of agonizing frustration.

I would propose also to bring to its test in these model units the much debated problem of how to keep more power of administrative decision down at the local level of the small self-contained unit. For any device to create more favorable conditions for direct participation of the citizen in the running of his community is essential for the attainment of an organic solution.

Nomadic Trend.   I remember that during a convention of the International Congress for Modern Architecture (CIAM) the question was raised by European architects whether Americans would ever be capable of creating a pattern for sound community life on a modern basis comparable to the closely knit townships that dominated the European picture before the advent of the machine. It was argued that the nomadic trend of the American population was so disruptive that nothing but makeshift arrangements could be expected and all local flavor would be destroyed by this mass of vacillating people in pursuit of the dollar. An American planner who was present * answered this challenge by telling of an experience he had had when he moved with his family to a place in Vermont that had always attracted him. He thought he had picked a town with the most pungent Vermont flavor, only to find, after some investigation, that the majority of the people were, like himself, born and raised elsewhere, but had selected Vermont as the place where they most wanted to live. They had come out of preference and had absorbed the local color to an astonishing degree. He felt that young Americans were not prepared to sit it out in the same towns where their parents and grandparents lived, as the Europeans have done for so many centuries; that, on the contrary, they usually became quite resentful when forced to do so. But, if given the chance to get around and look at as many regions as possible, they finally picked out one to settle down in permanently which for various reasons appealed most to them and then often became more co-operative and enter-

* Martin Meyerson, Assistant Professor of City Planning, University of Pennsylvania.

prising citizens than those who had never stirred from home. Now, if we can conceive of the future citizen as a person willing to contribute wherever he happens to settle down instead of merely looking for the easiest opening and the quickest gain, then we have, maybe, found an answer to this baffling spectacle of a nation whose citizens are, voluntarily or involuntarily, so much on the move.

To help this development we must conceive contemporary community features which would exert so stimulating an influence on the citizen who comes to live there that he will soon change from an onlooker into a participator. Such a desirable trend could well be brought about by a campaign to recapture the right-of-way for the pedestrian. As we all know, every citizen is both, now a driver, now a pedestrian; but while everything is being done for the car and its driver, the pedestrian has been pushed against the wall in the process of building up the great net of automotive traffic which has exploded our communities. I am convinced that it is just as necessary, or even more so, now to create, in addition, independent pedestrian traffic nets, separate and protected from the automobile. Such a superimposed pedestrian path pattern should start and end, not at a strung-out main street, but in a beautiful plaza, prohibited for cars, the very heart or core of the unit, to serve as the local center for the exchange of public opinion and participation in community affairs. Here, from daily social intercourse in trade and recreation, from gossip on local and world news, grow the grass roots of politics. Such a pedestrian square of human scale with its centralized social purpose would give the inhabitant a feeling of belonging and pride. It would prepare him for the sharing of responsibility, for conscientious voting and for his taking an interest in community planning which the planner needs so badly for future action. This is an ardent plea for the modern community core, the most vital organ to promote democratic process.

Human Scale for the City.   I so strongly emphasize the small self-contained unit with its community center because new experience here, on the smallest scale, will throw new light also on the more complicated problem of the larger cities and the metropolis. It will help in the gigantic task of humanizing them. For the problem of the big cities is certainly not one of building only new civic centers or piece-meal housing. It is evident that nothing less than a complete overhaul of their sclerotic bodies can turn them into healthy organisms again. We all know that their congested areas are hungry for open spaces, for nature, light and air, that their citizens long for a recognition of their identity, while the city itself needs to be protected at the same time against individual encroachment. I do not intend to elaborate on the social, political and economic procedures and implementations to reach this goal. But I wish to stress the great need of more systematic research also on the metropolitan level. How can we recapture in the city, socially and physically, the completely destroyed human scale? Research has to precede the necessary action. The growth of a living urban organism can be channeled into a superior civic form by the planner and architect only if its social functions have been recognized by new legislation, built up on the results of that preceding research. Existing law is mostly obsolete and insufficient for twentieth-century urban life, and most countries have as yet failed to put the emphasis on the whole of the communal organism, on its context rather than on its separate parts.

"Housing" Is Not Enough. If we try to appraise the physical achievements in housing and in organic community setup during the last twenty years, we can safely state that in several countries plan and construction of the individual family dwelling or apartment has been greatly improved with respect to livability and level of standard, but there is hardly any so-called "development" which would appeal to us as a true community, balanced in itself. Developments usually show just a quantity of streets and houses, accumulated in an additive manner without such communal features as would transform a mere housing scheme into a purposely limited, well-sized organism. They may be made up of pleasant, individual houses and often present an admirable economical achievement, but the layout of the town is usually but a dull, unimaginative conglomeration of endless strings of houses. It utterly lacks the stimulation that might have been attained from those intangibles of creative beautiful design and total conception which give life its deeper value and for which the past has given us magnificent examples of unity.

As to the conception of the contemporary dwelling itself we must first start by checking up on our own attitude toward the human and psychological components of the problem and its ever changing aspects. Only a mature mind with deep understanding of the physical and psychological requirements of family life is able to conceive a shell for living to be efficient, inexpensive, beautiful and so flexible that it will be adequate for the ever changing life cycle of the family in all its stages of growth.

Our Habitat. However, the greatest responsibility of the planner and architect, I believe, is the protection and development of our habitat. Man has evolved a mutual relationship with nature on earth, but his power to change its surface has grown so tremendously that this may become a curse instead of a blessing. How can we afford to have one beautiful tract of open country after the other bulldozed out of existence, flattened and emptied for the sake of smooth building operations and then filled up by a developer with hundreds of insipid little house units, that will never grow into a community, and scores of telephone poles added in place of the thoughtlessly cut trees? Native vegetation and the natural irregularities of the topography are destroyed by negligence, greed or lack of ideas, because the average type of developer regards the land first of all as a commercial commodity from which he feels entitled to reap a maximum profit. *Until we love and respect the land almost religiously, its fatal deterioration will go on.*

The human landscape which surrounds us is a broad composition in space, organized from voids and volumes. The volumes may be buildings or bridges or trees or hills. Every visible feature in existence, natural or man-made, counts in the visual effect of that great composition. Even the most utilitarian building problems, like the location of a highway or the type of a bridge, are important for the integrated balance of that visible entity which surrounds us. Who else but the creative planner and architect should be the legitimate, responsible guardian for our most precious possession, our natural habitat, for the beauty and adequateness of our living space as a source of emotional satisfaction for a new way of life? What all of us seem to need most in this hectic rush we have let life slide into is an ubiquitous source of regeneration which can be only nature herself. Under trees the urban dweller might restore his troubled soul and find the blessing of a creative pause.

I have come to the conclusion that an architect or planner worth the name must have a very broad and comprehensive vision indeed to achieve a true synthesis of a future community. This we might call "total architecture." To do such a total job he needs the ardent passion of a lover and the humble willingness to collaborate with others, for great as he may be he cannot do it alone. The kinship of regional architectural expression which we so much desire will greatly depend, I believe, on the creative development of teamwork. Abandoning the morbid hunt for "styles" we have already started to develop together certain attitudes and principles which reflect the new way of life of twentieth-century man. *We have begun to understand that designing our physical environment does not mean to apply a fixed set of esthetics, but embodies rather a continuous inner growth, a conviction which recreates truth continually in the service of mankind.*

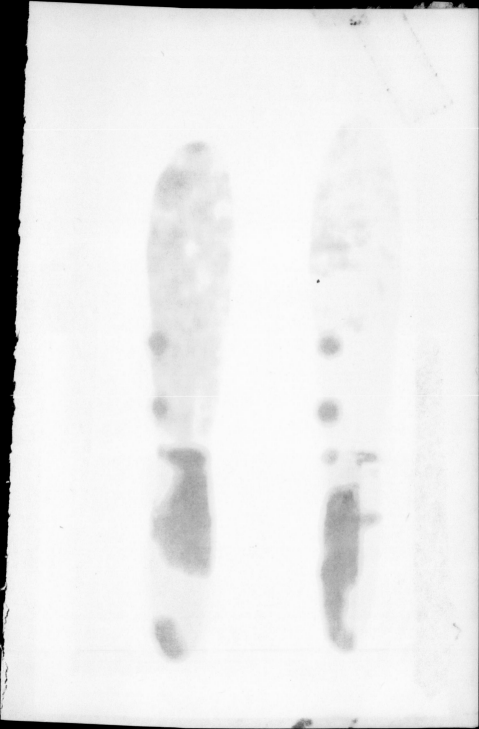

5/6/55

35572

NA
680
G73

GROPIUS, WALTER
    SCOPE OF TOTAL
ARCHITECTURE

DATE DUE

DEC 0 2 2001	

Fernald Library
Colby-Sawyer College
New London, New Hampshire

GAYLORD   PRINTED IN U.S.A.